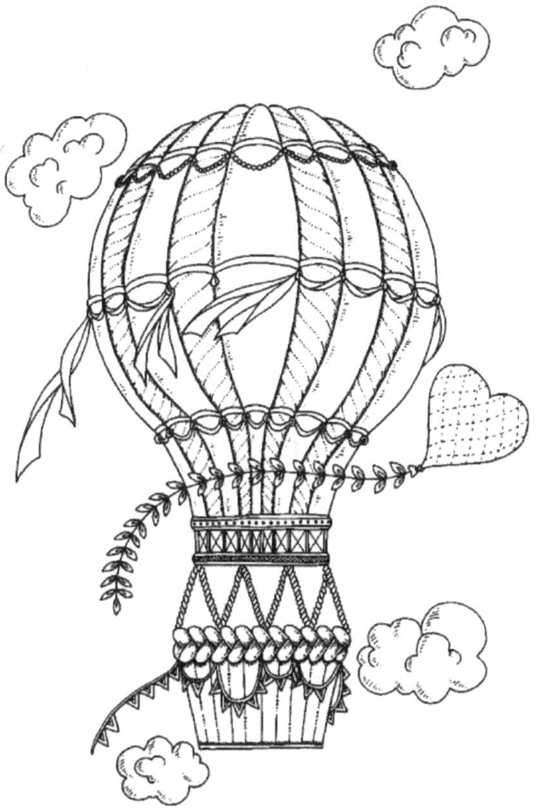

BALLOON PUBLISHING

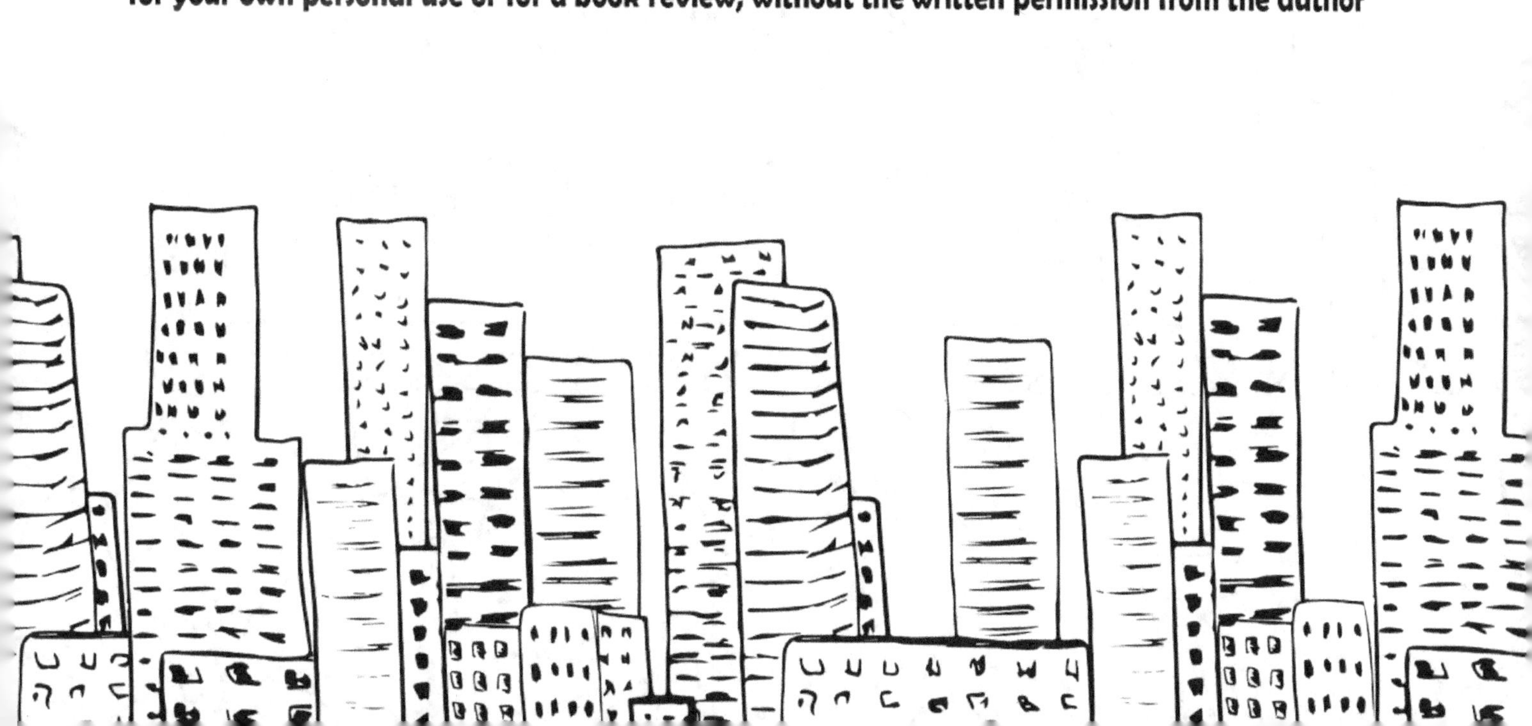

COLOR TEST PAGE

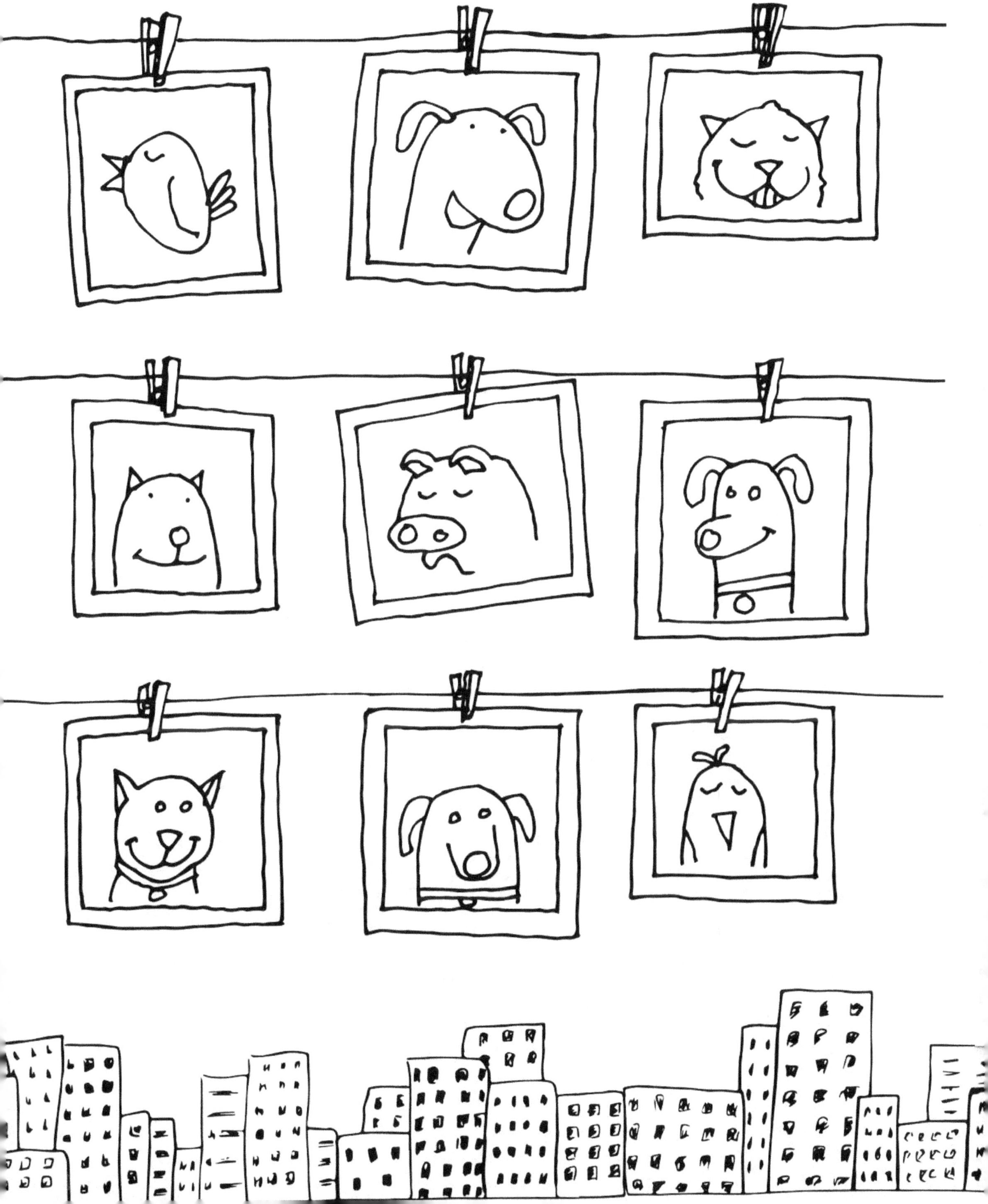

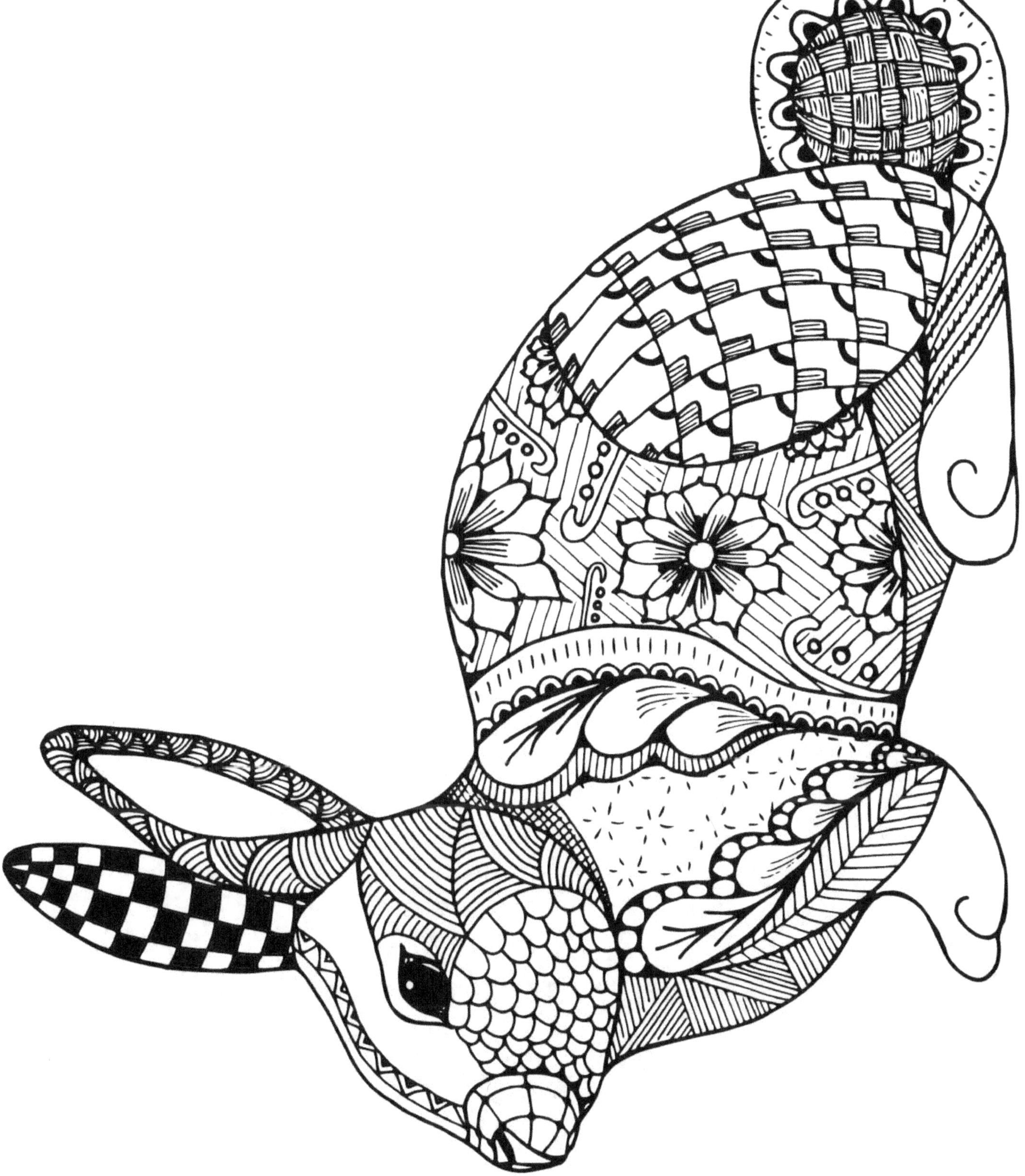

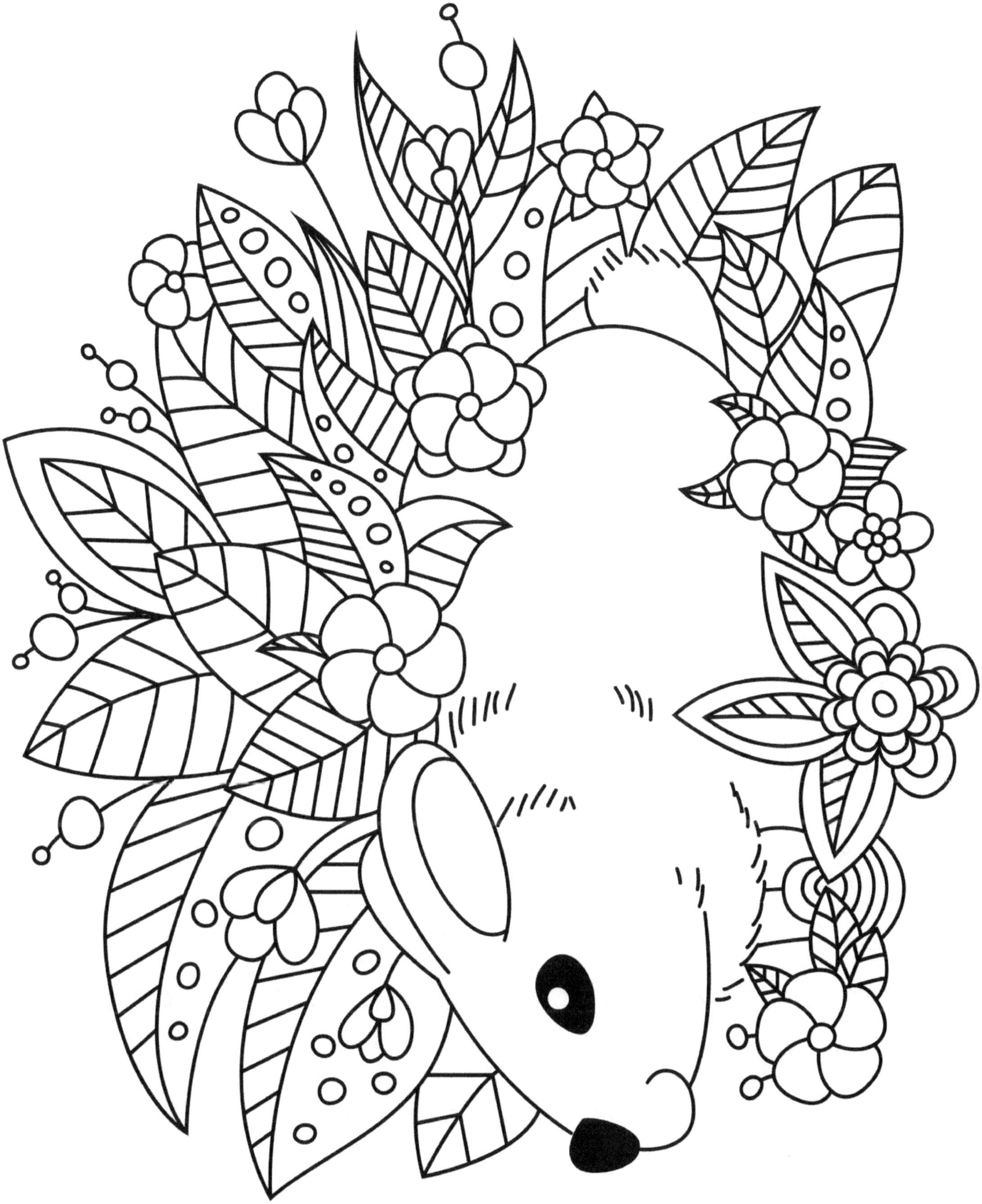

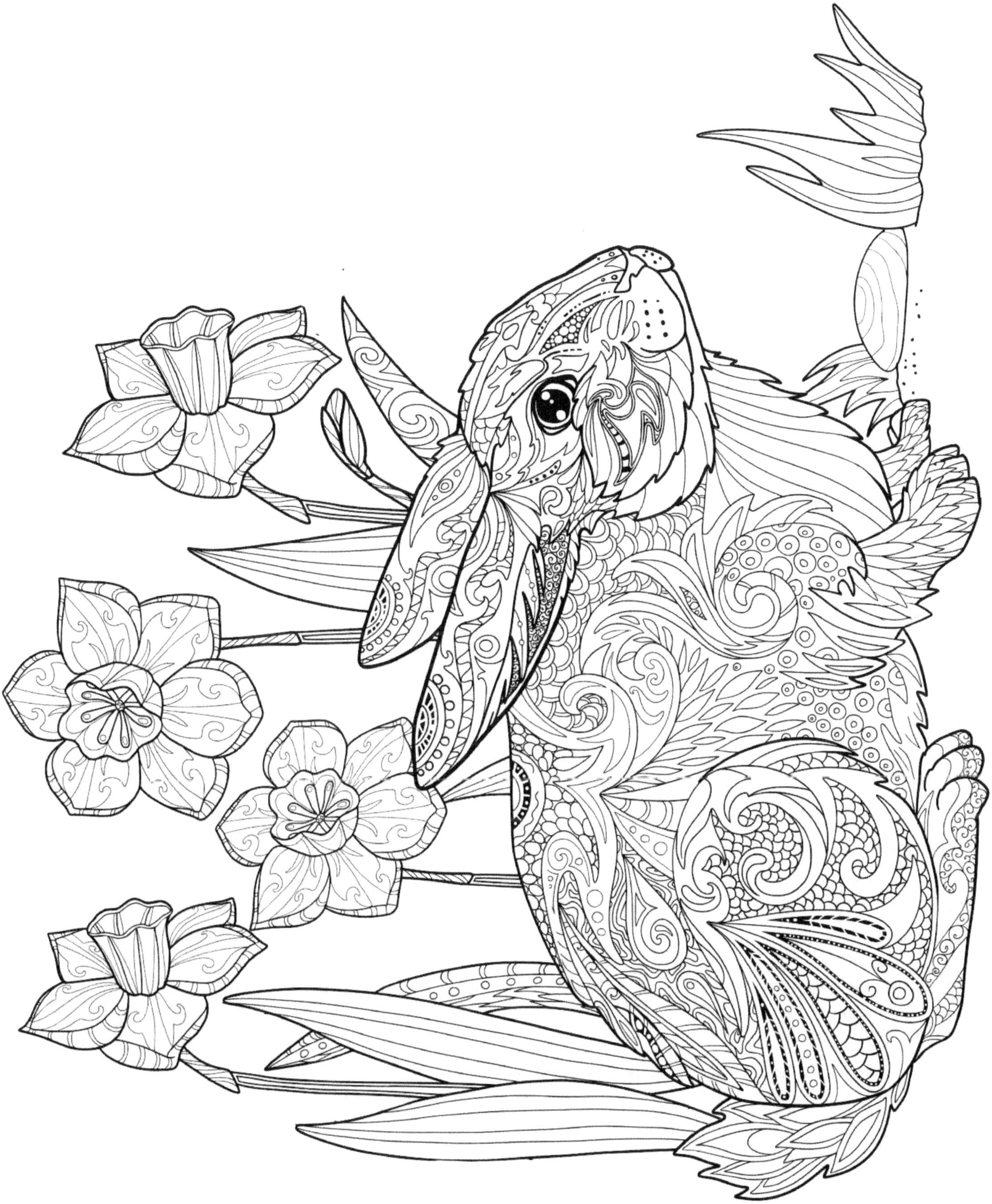

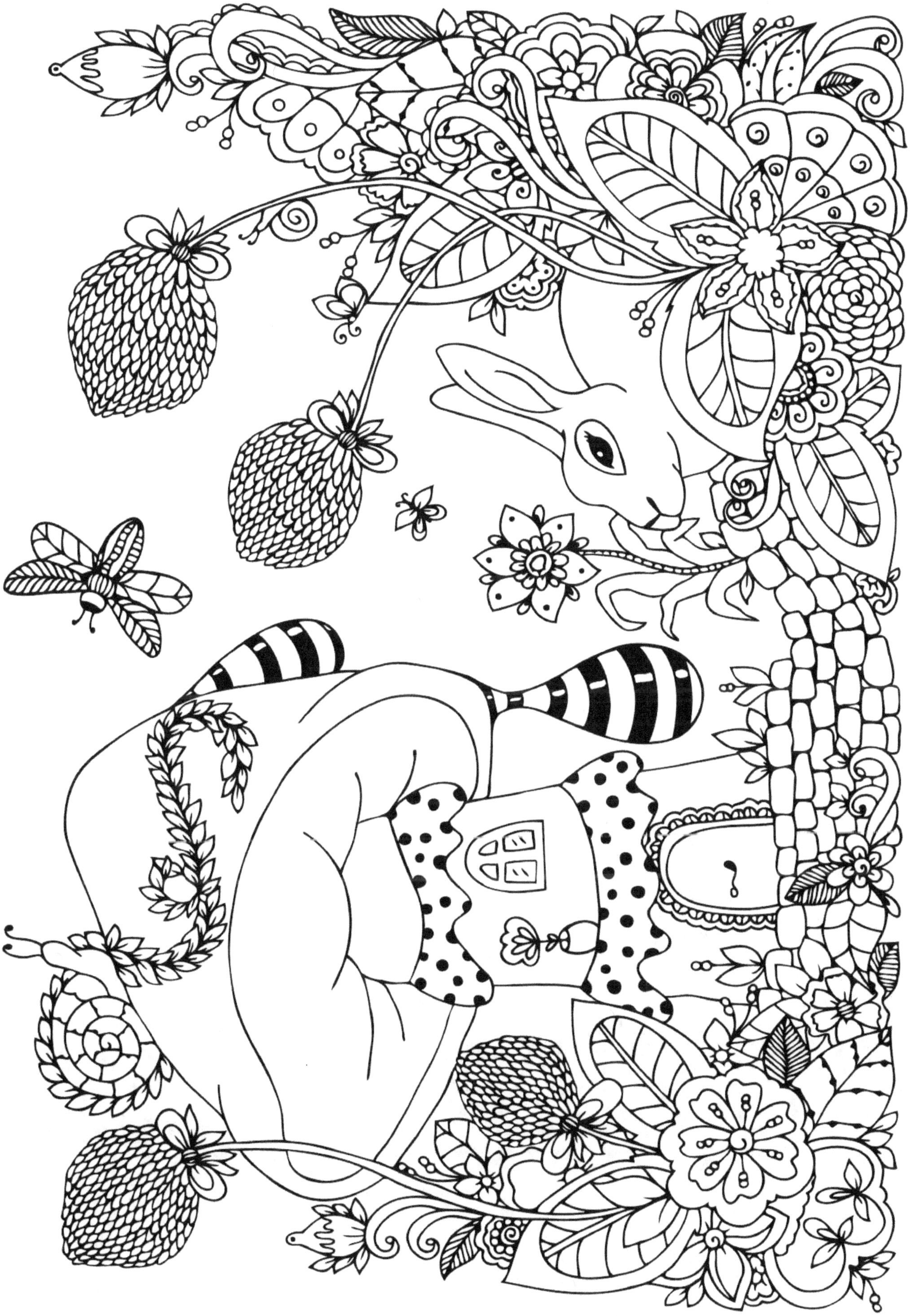

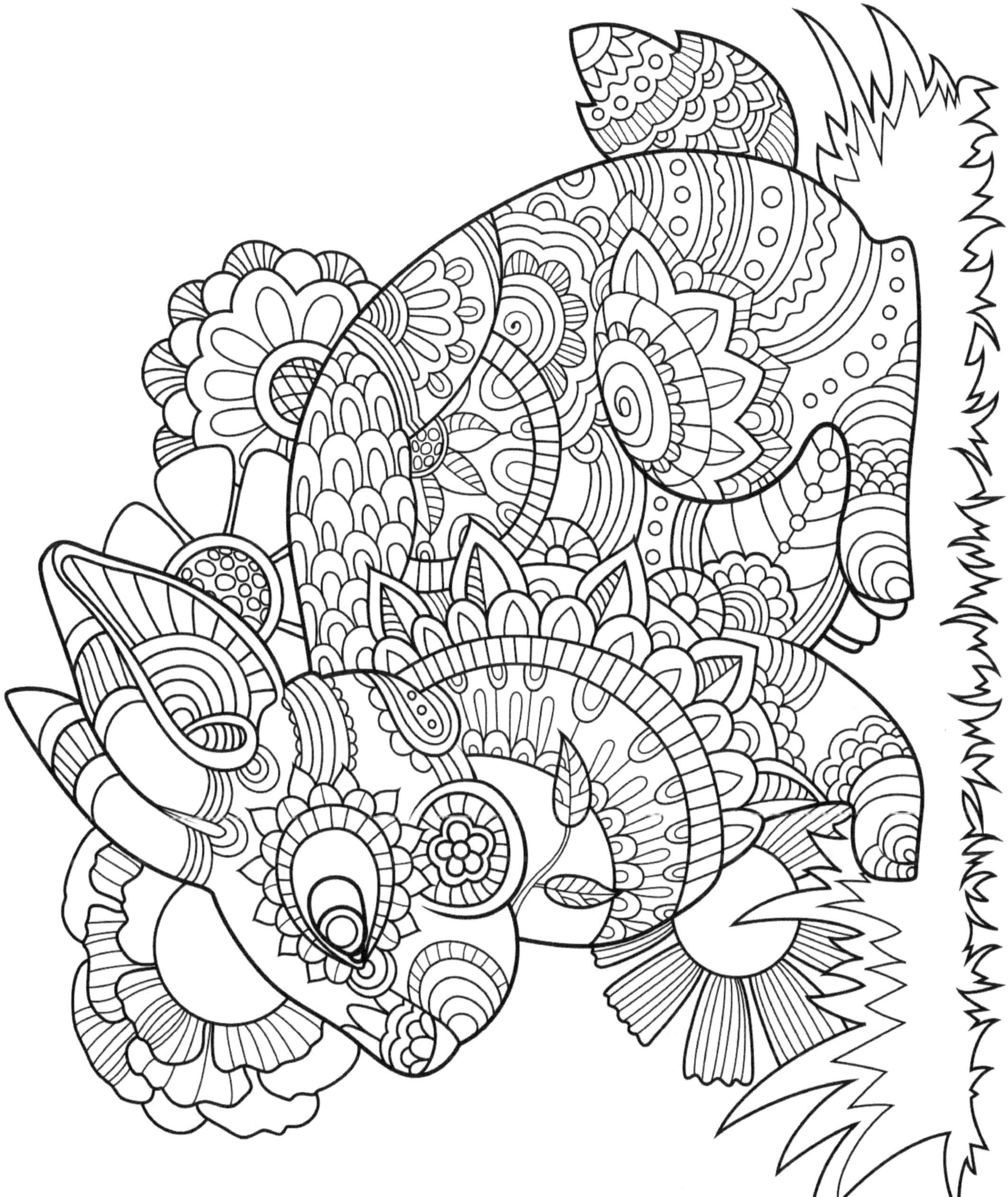

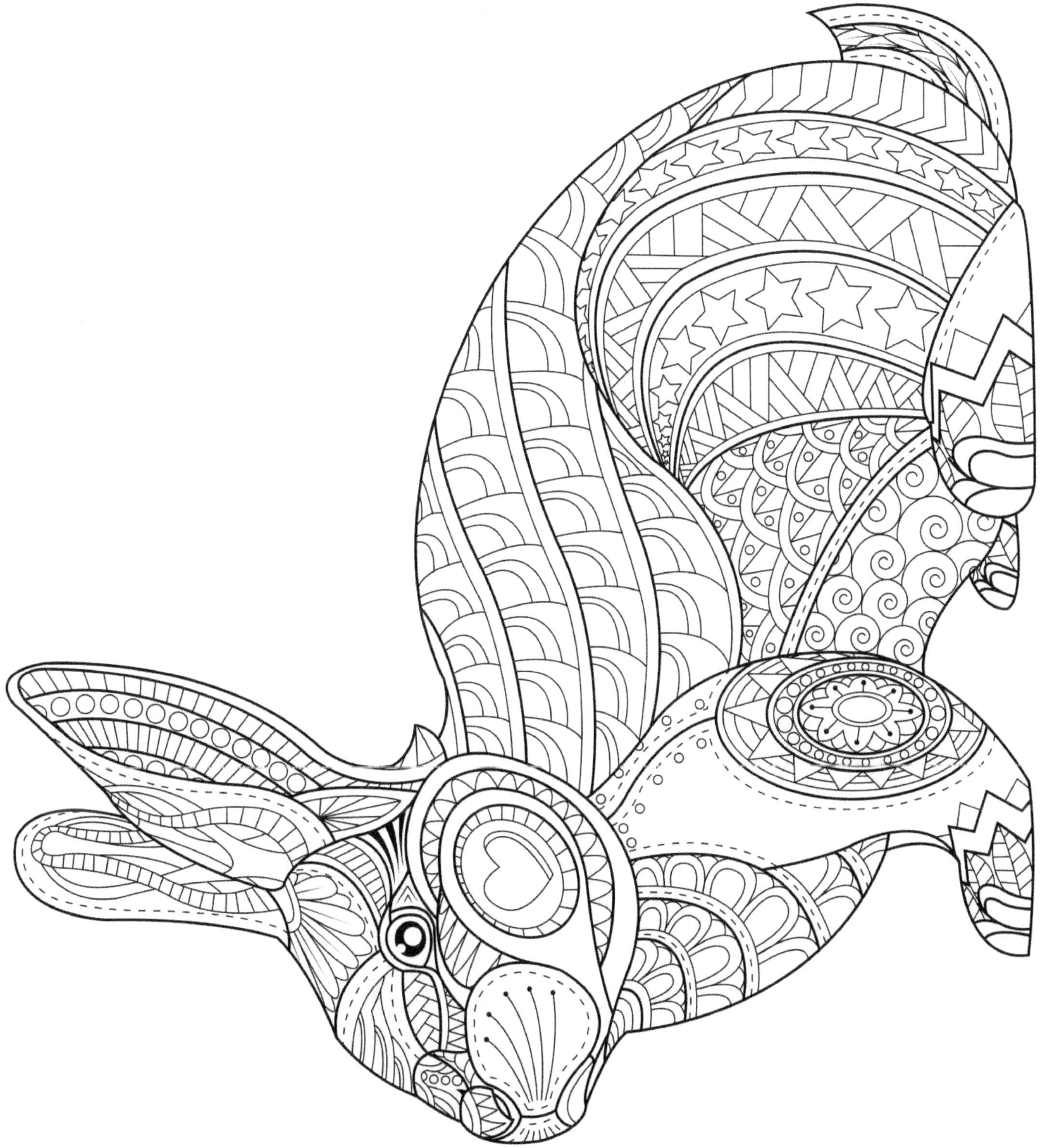

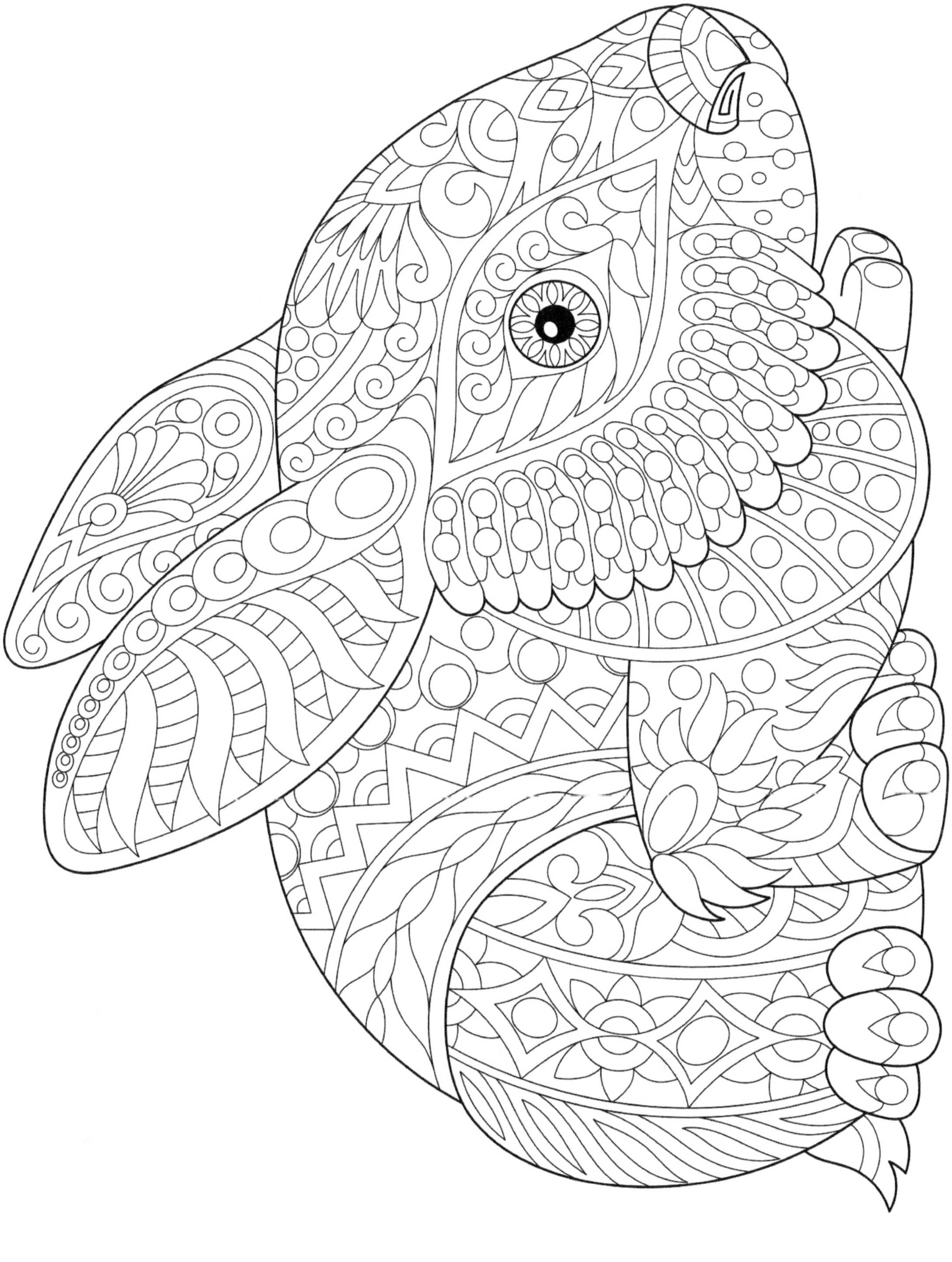

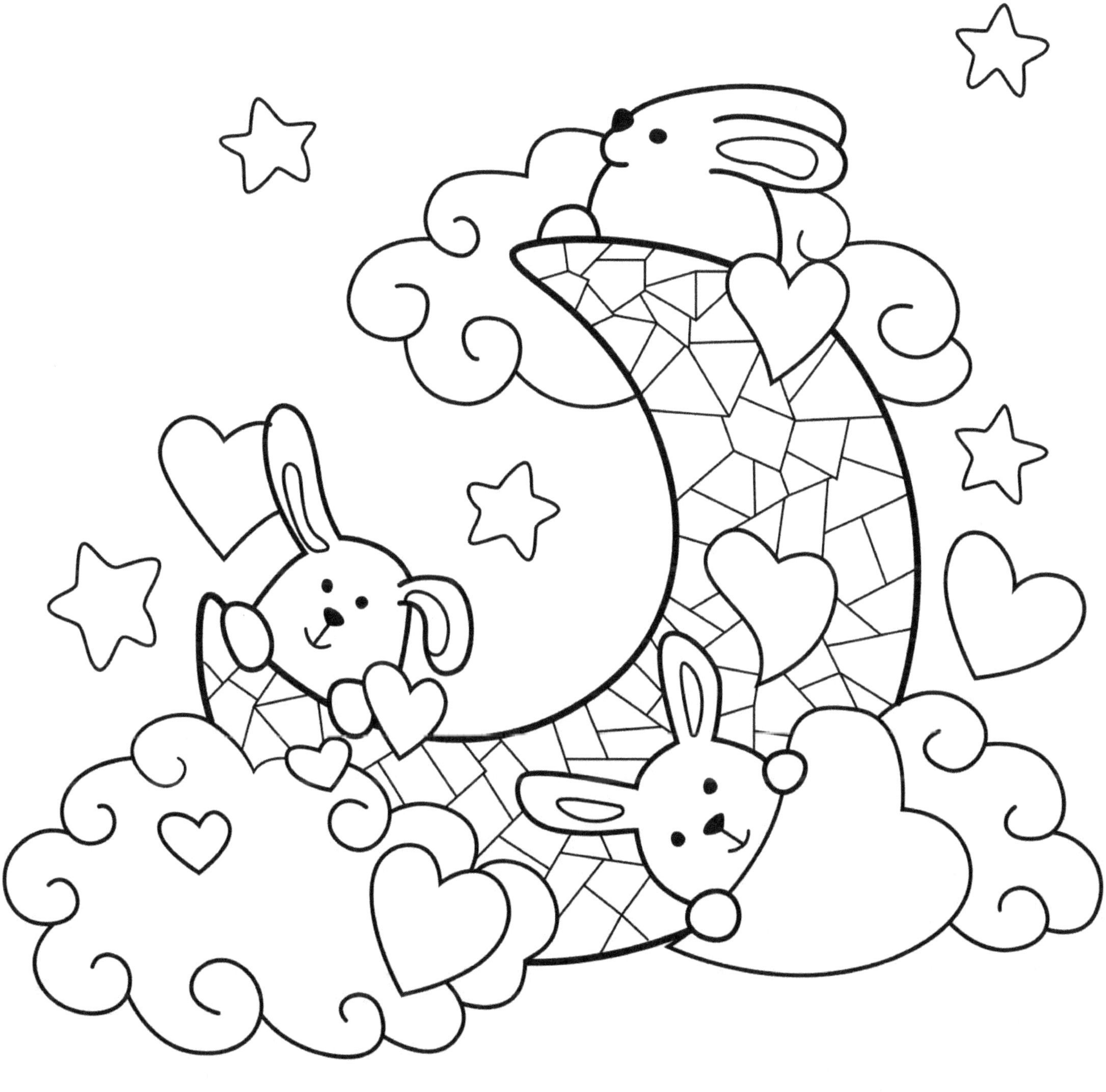

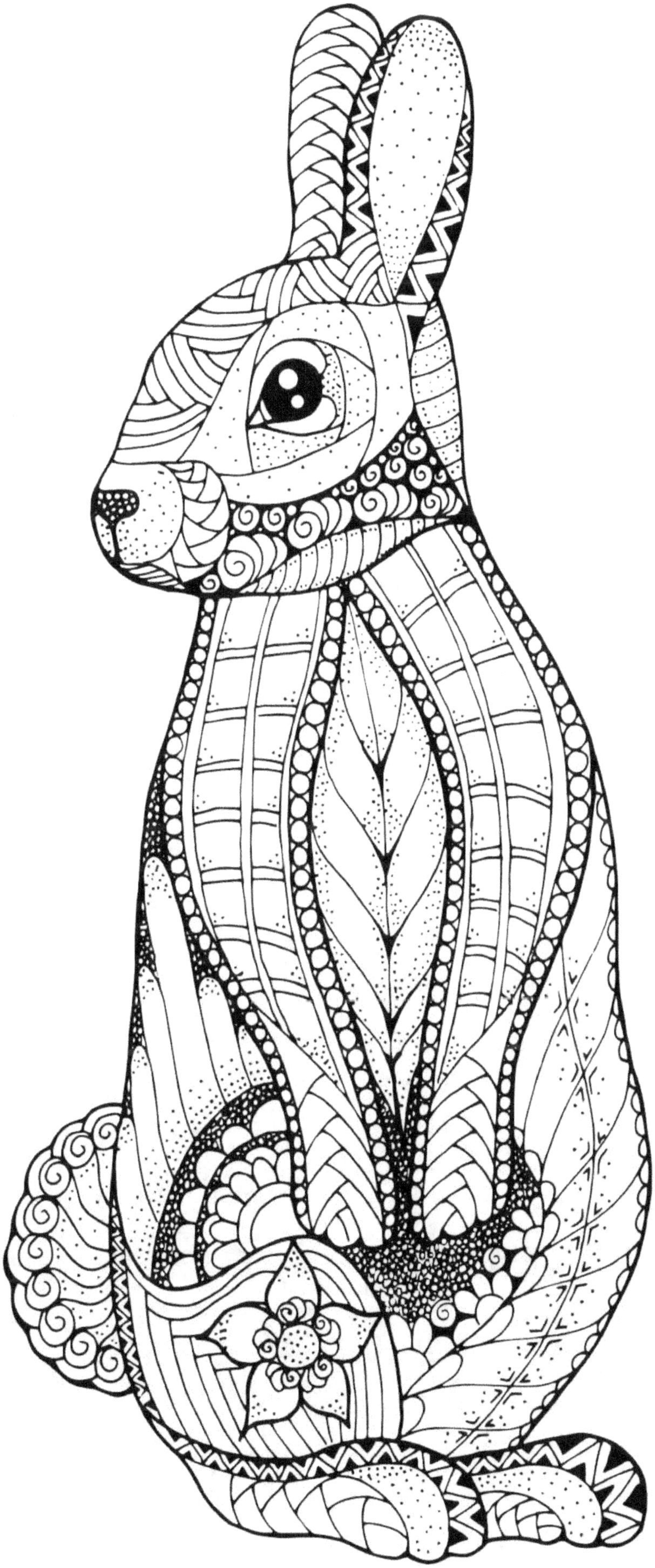

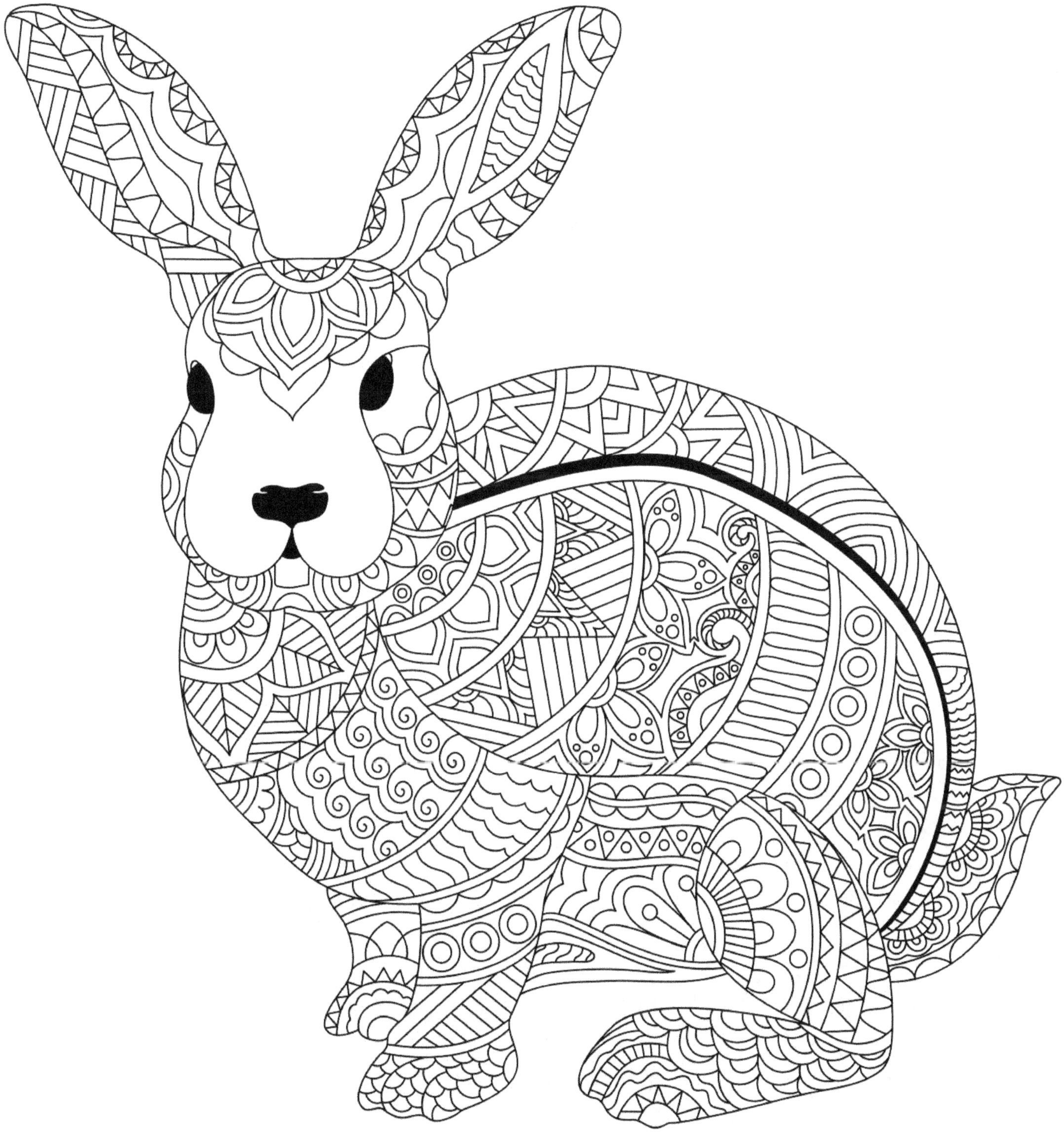

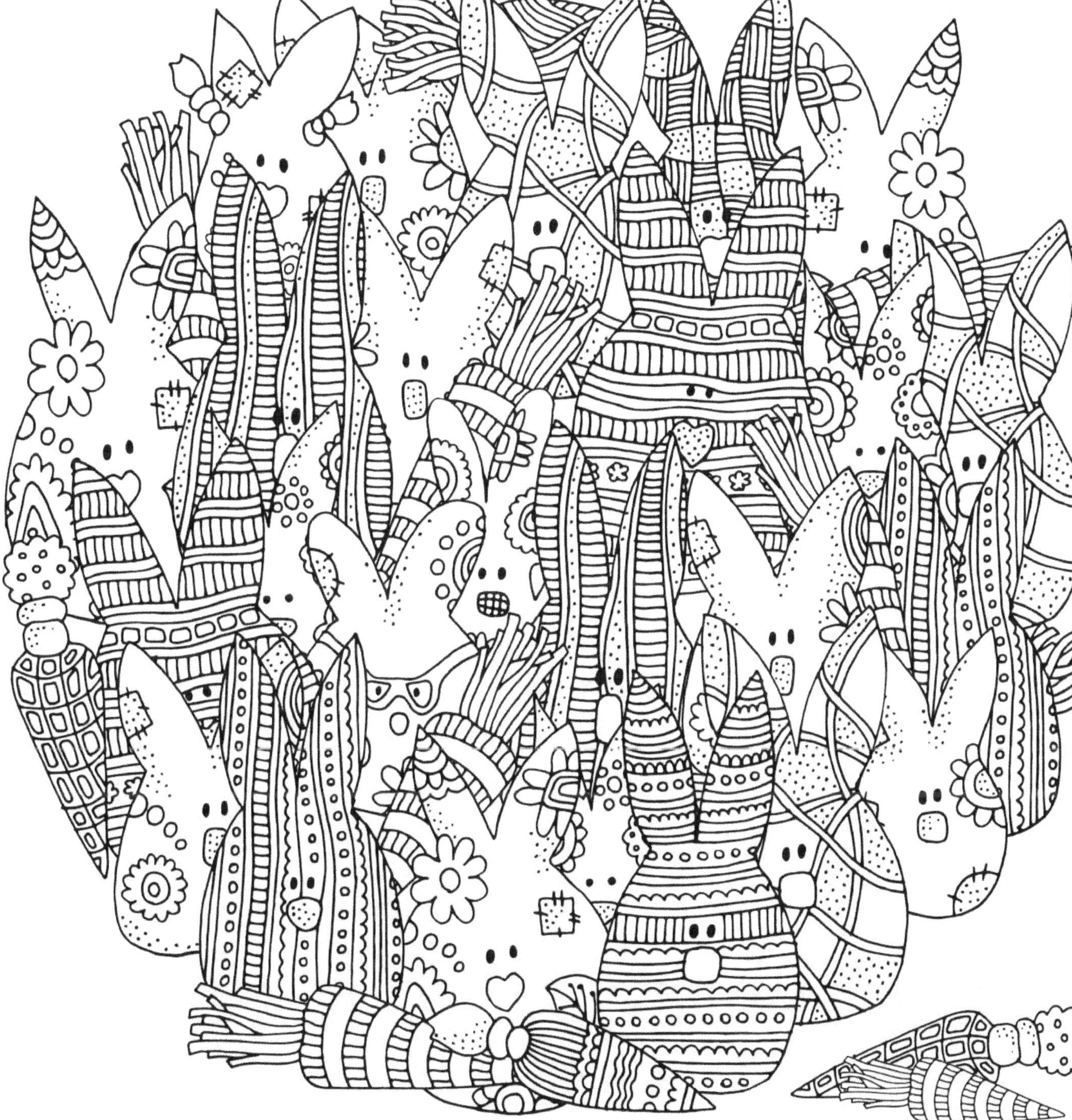

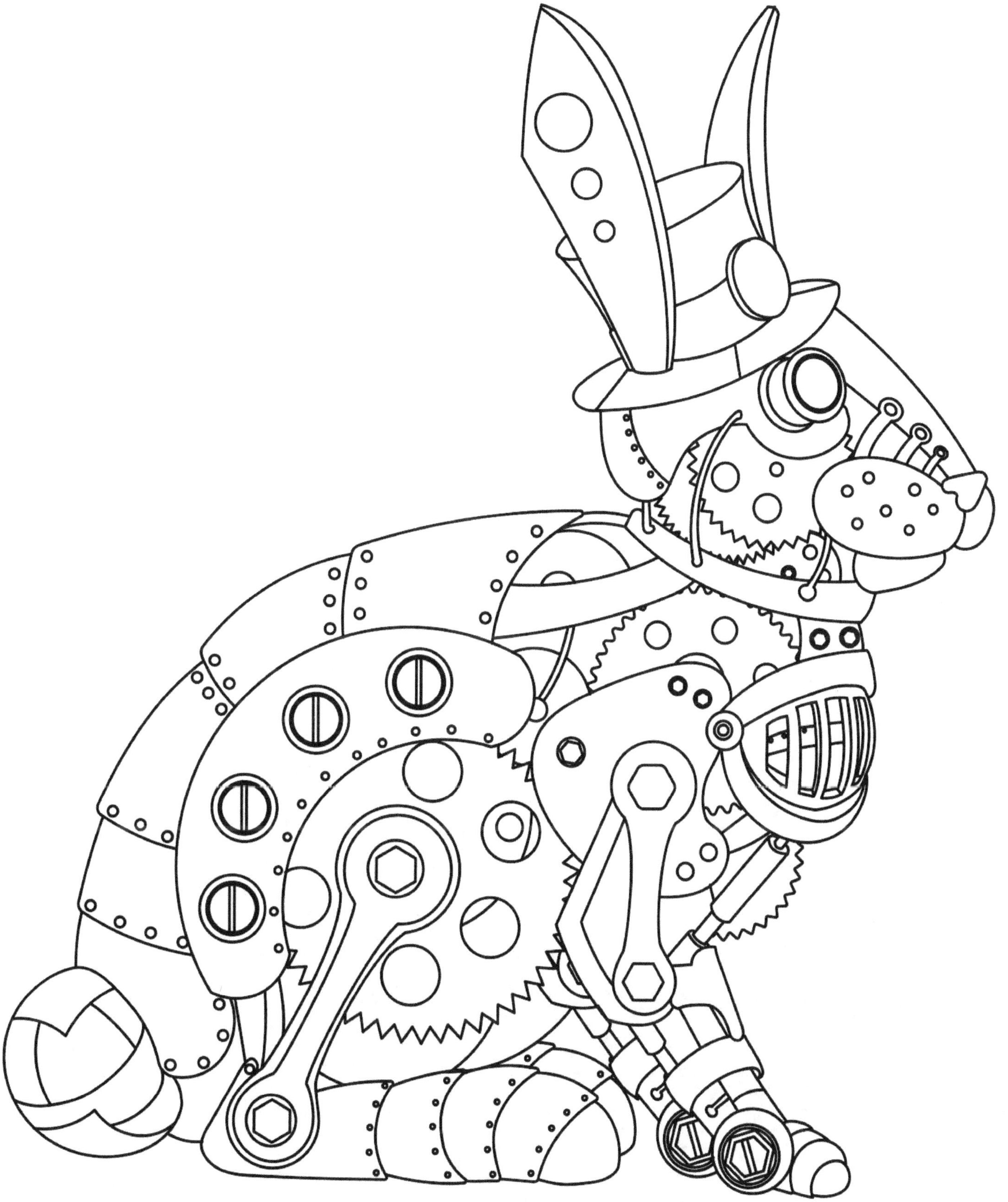

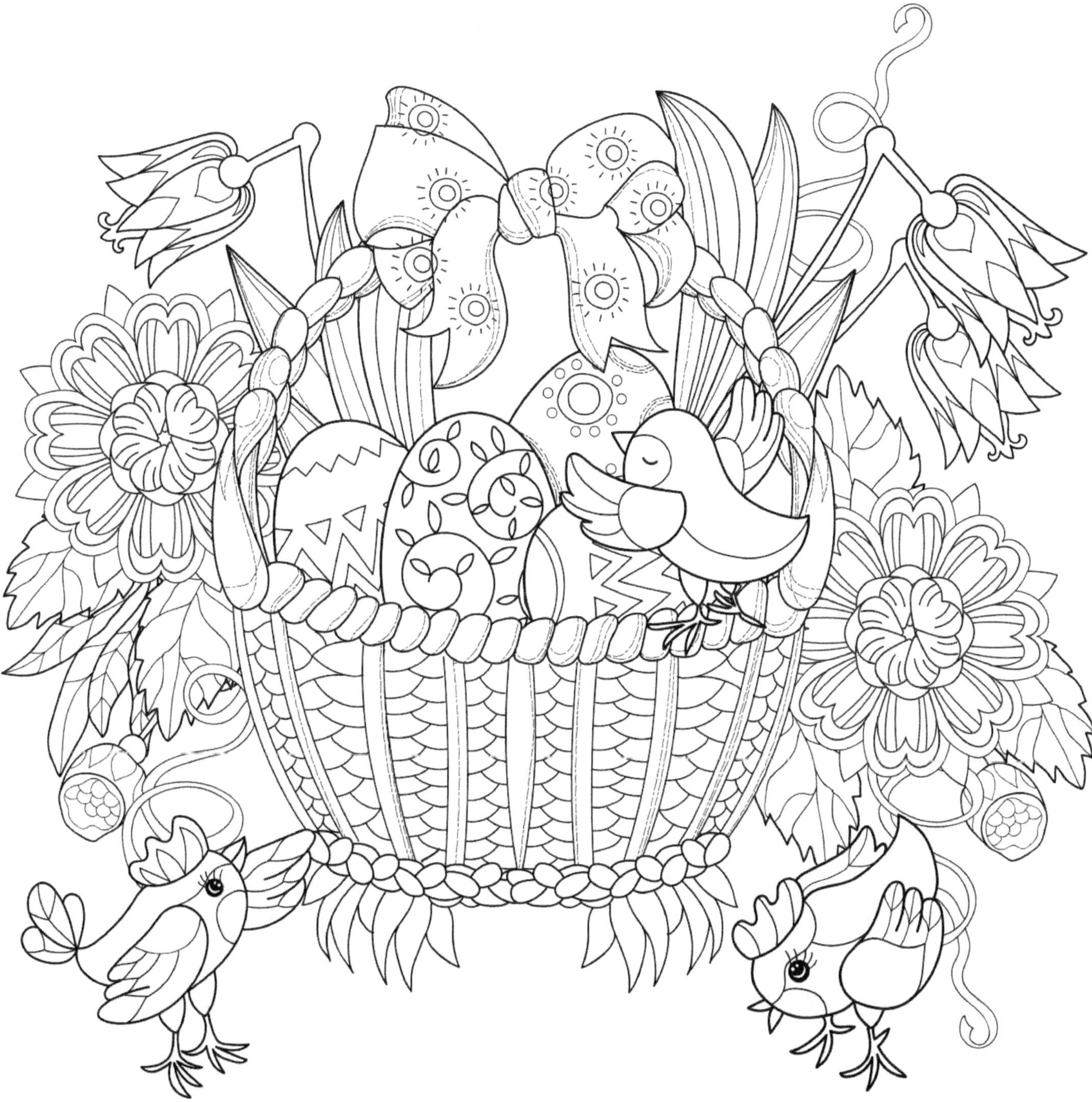

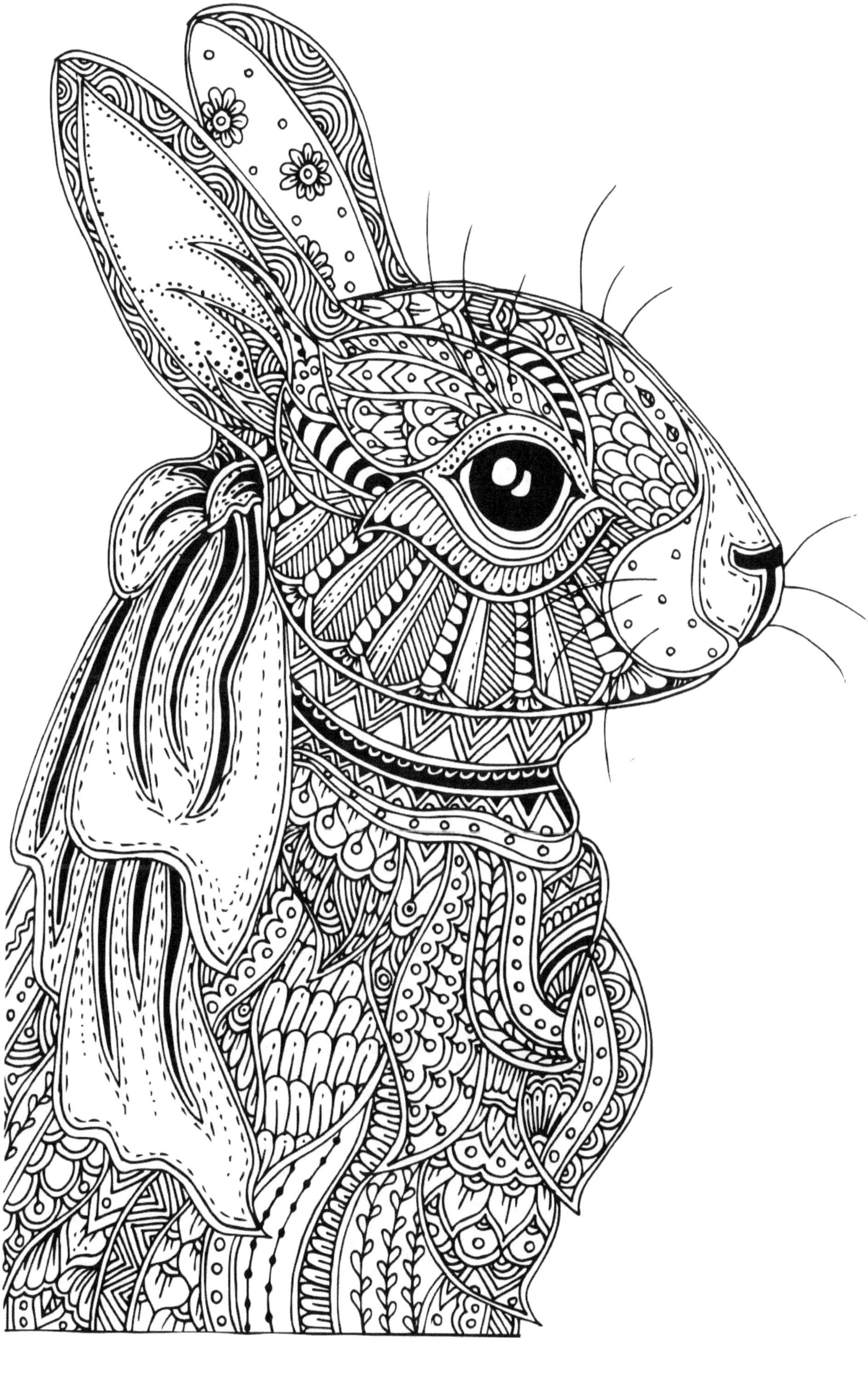

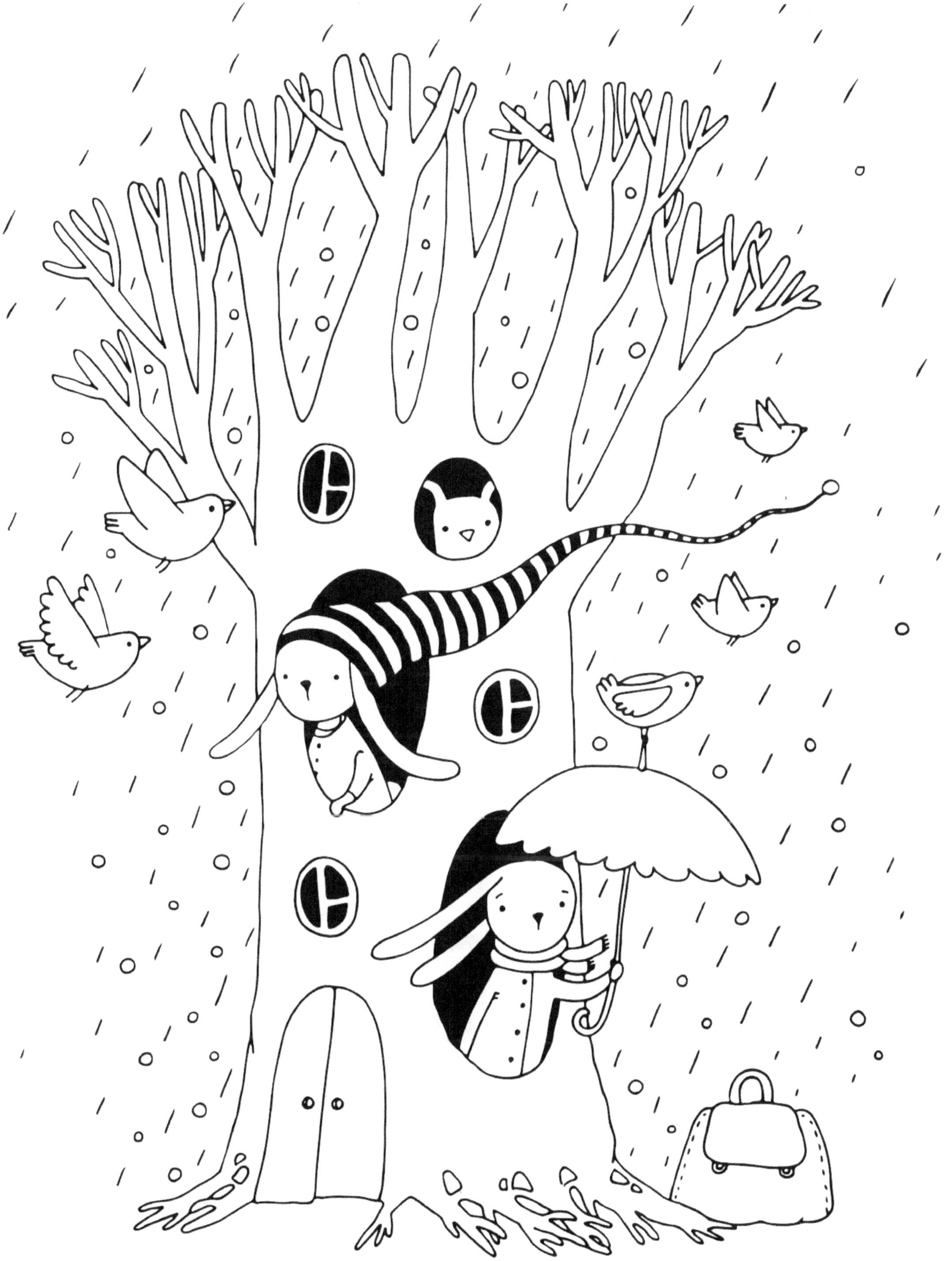

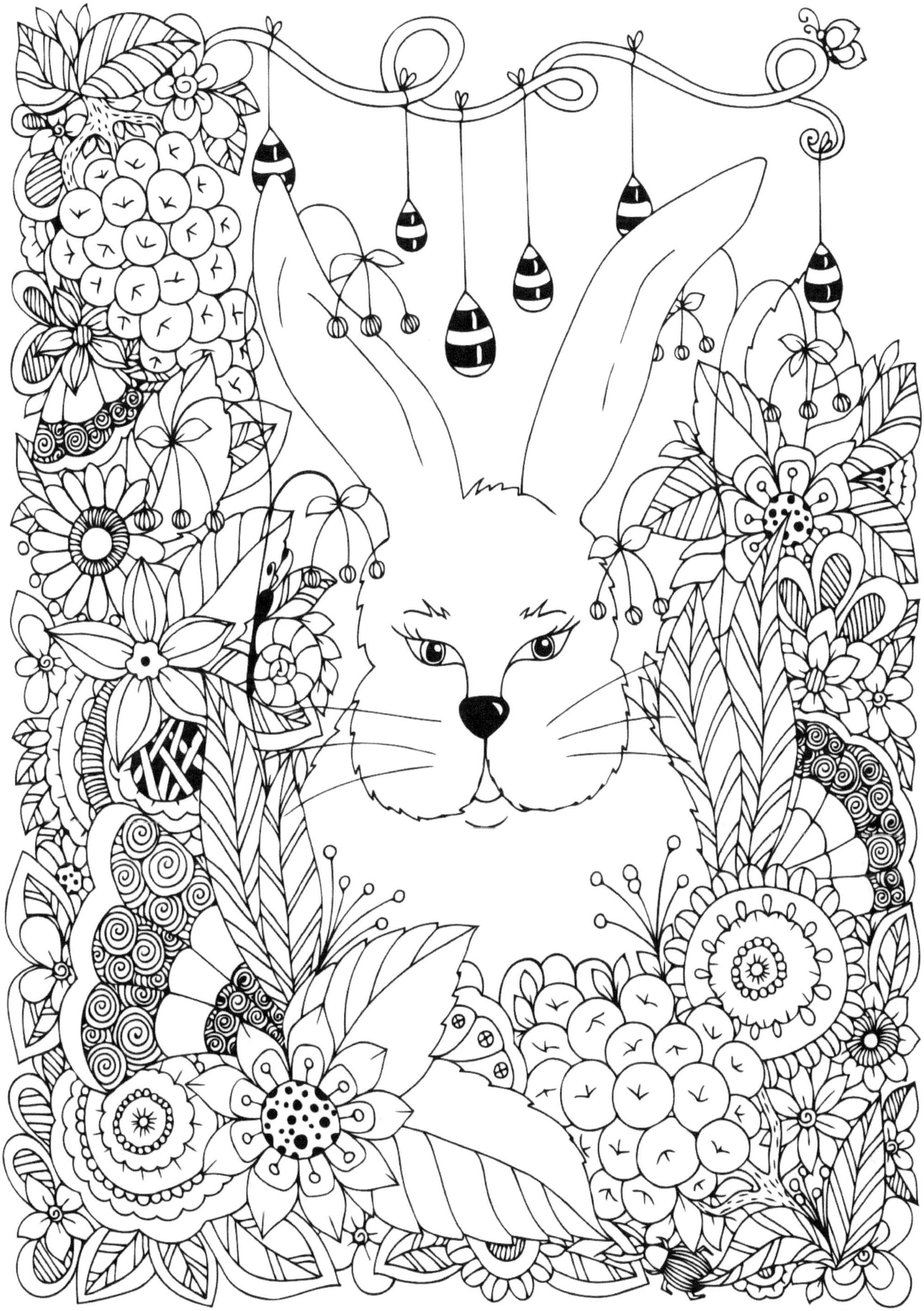

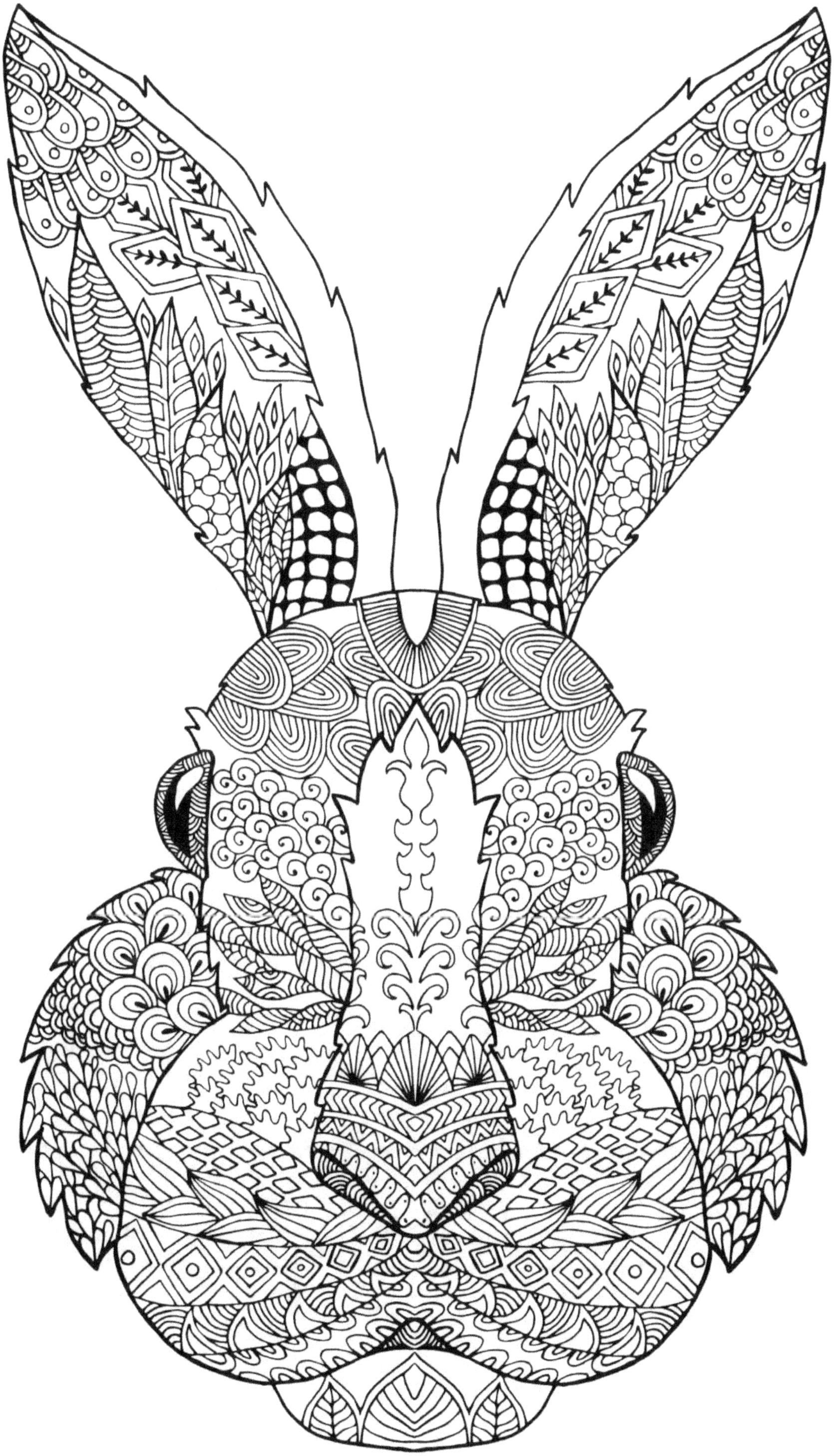

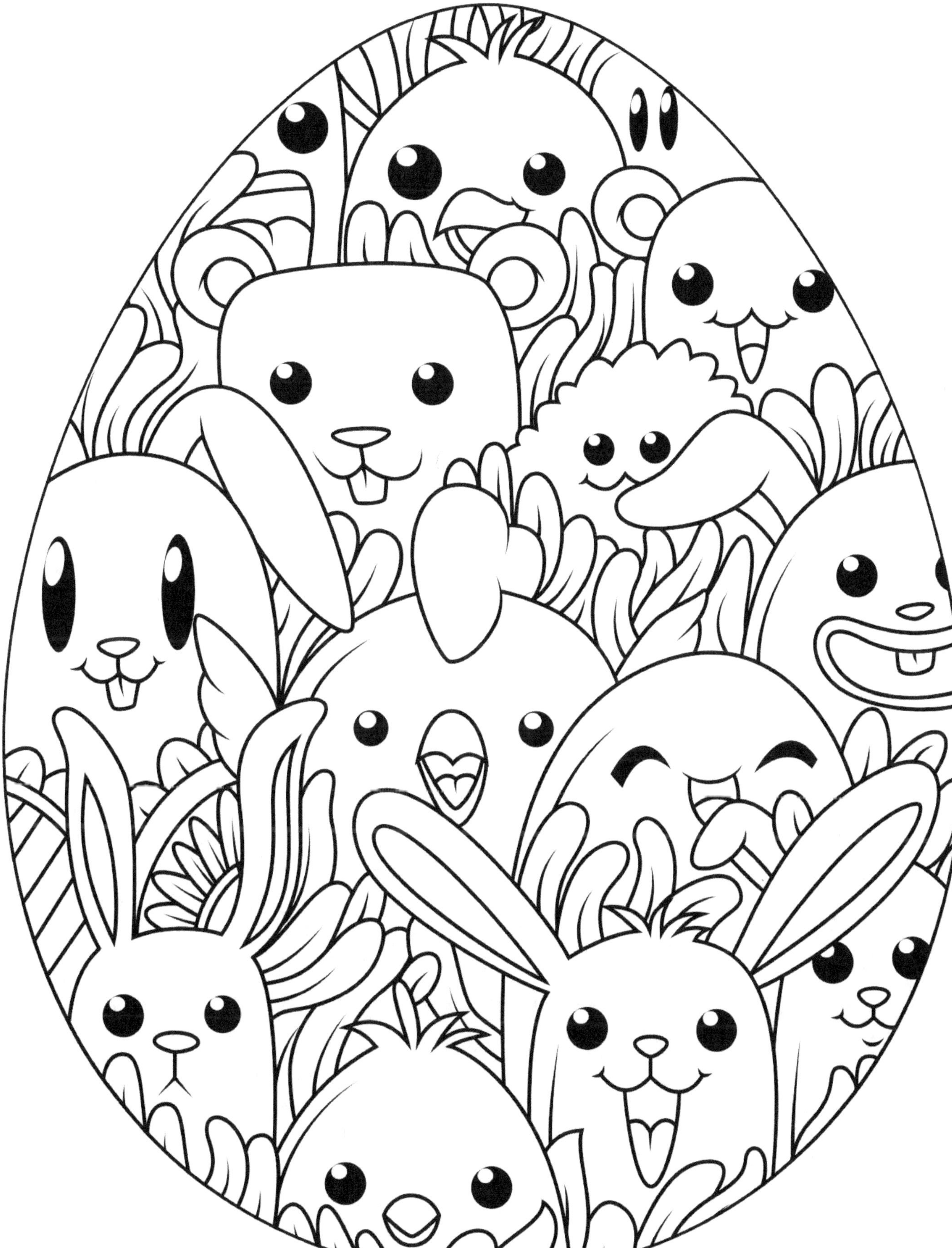

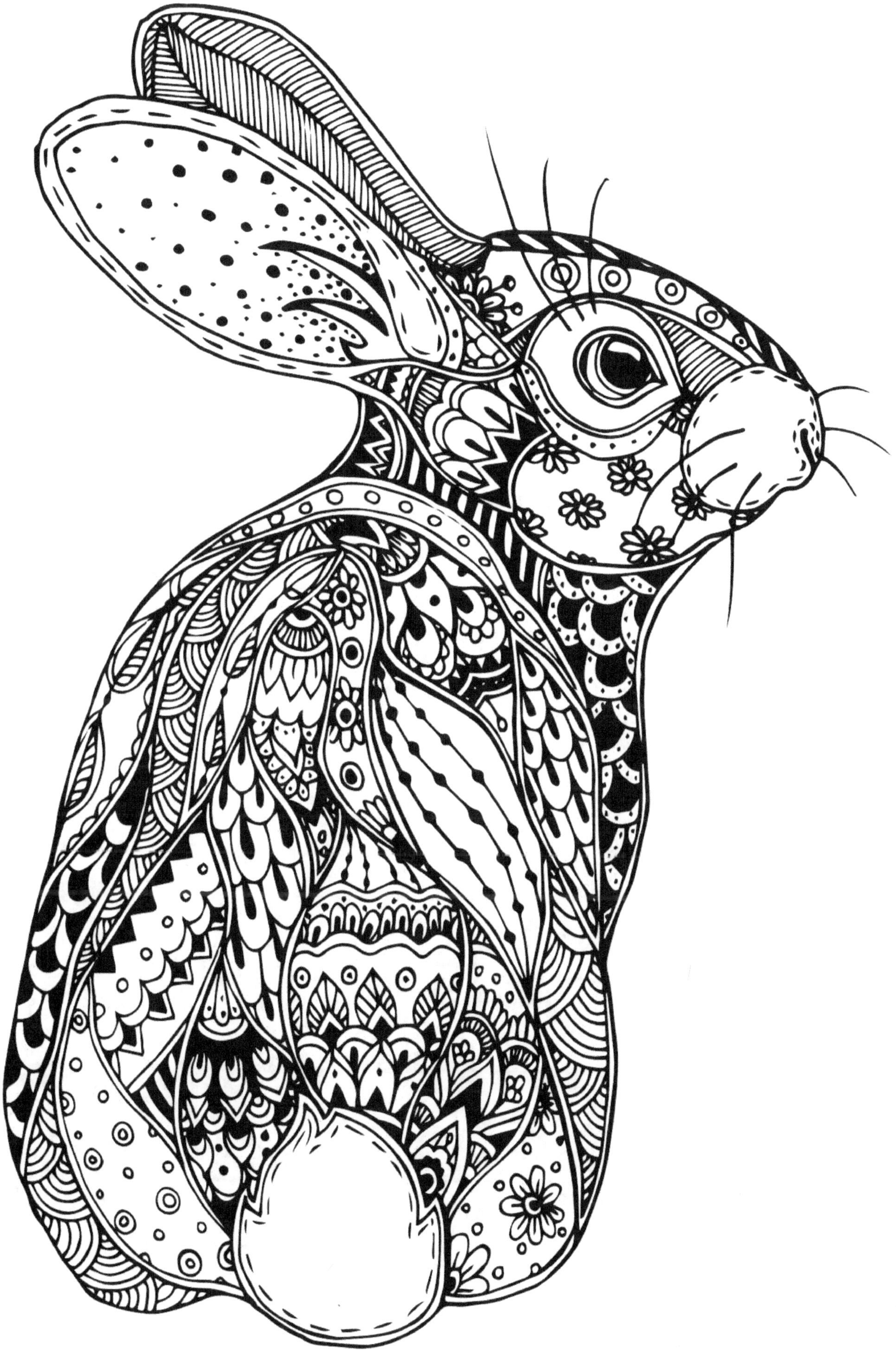

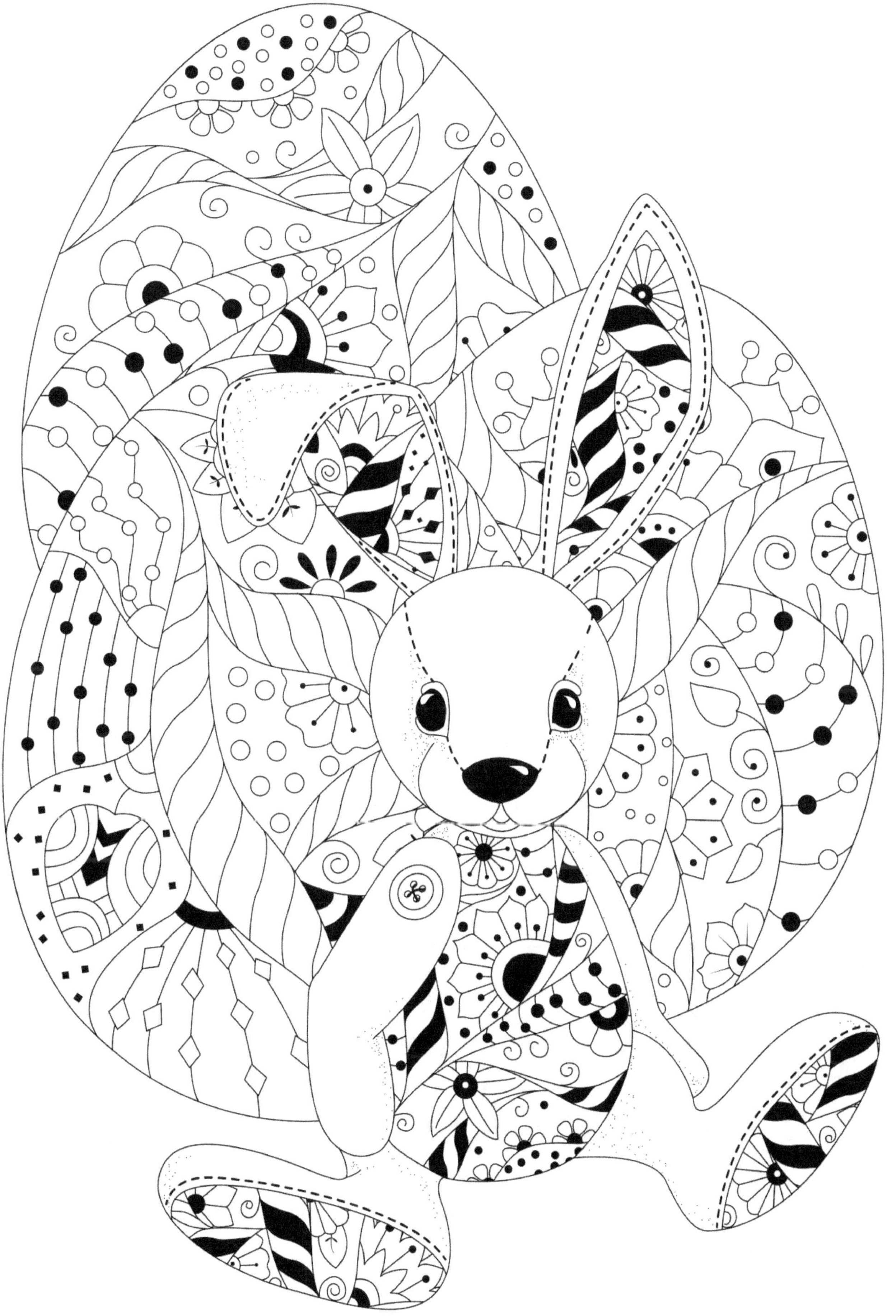

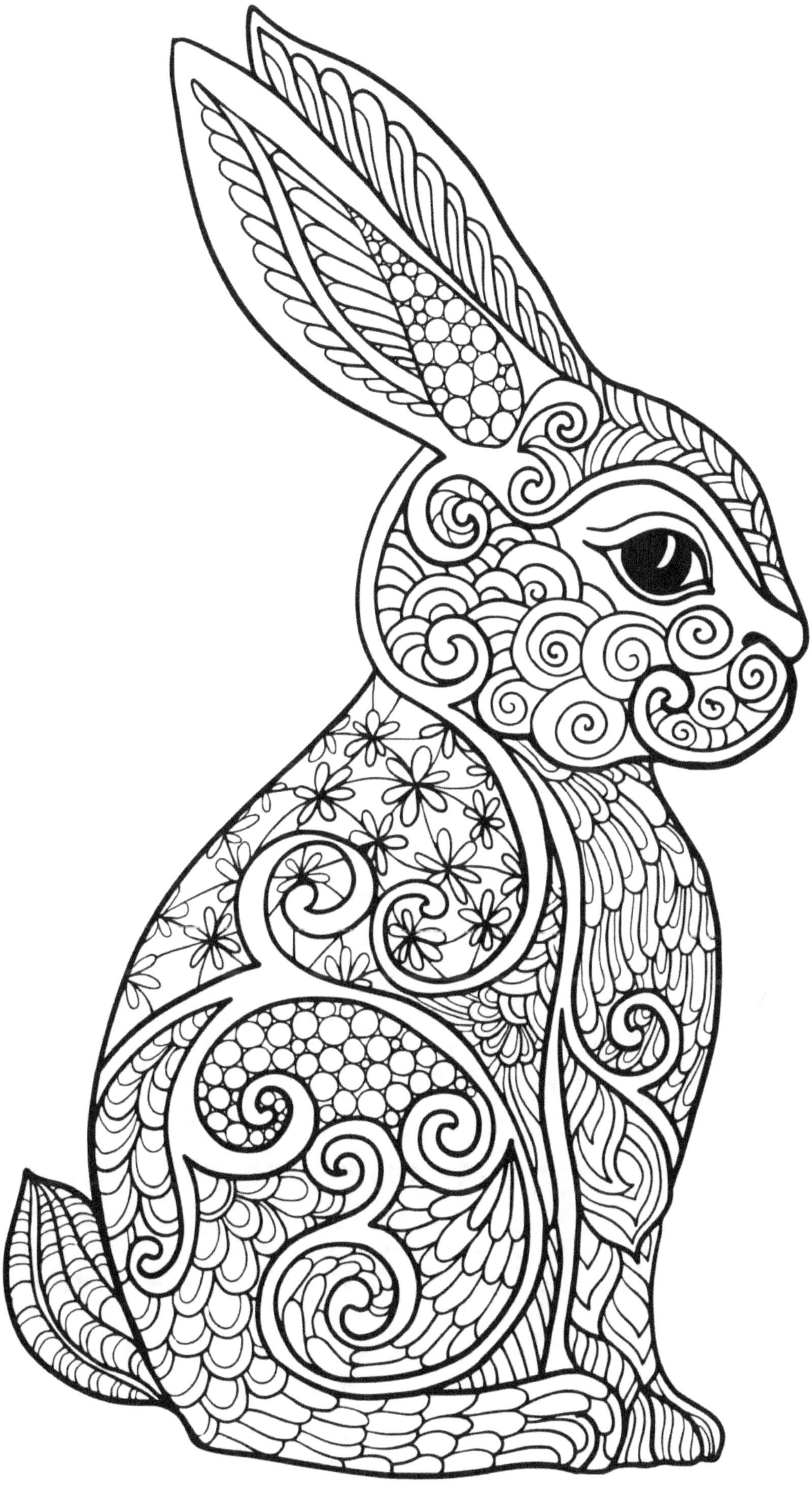

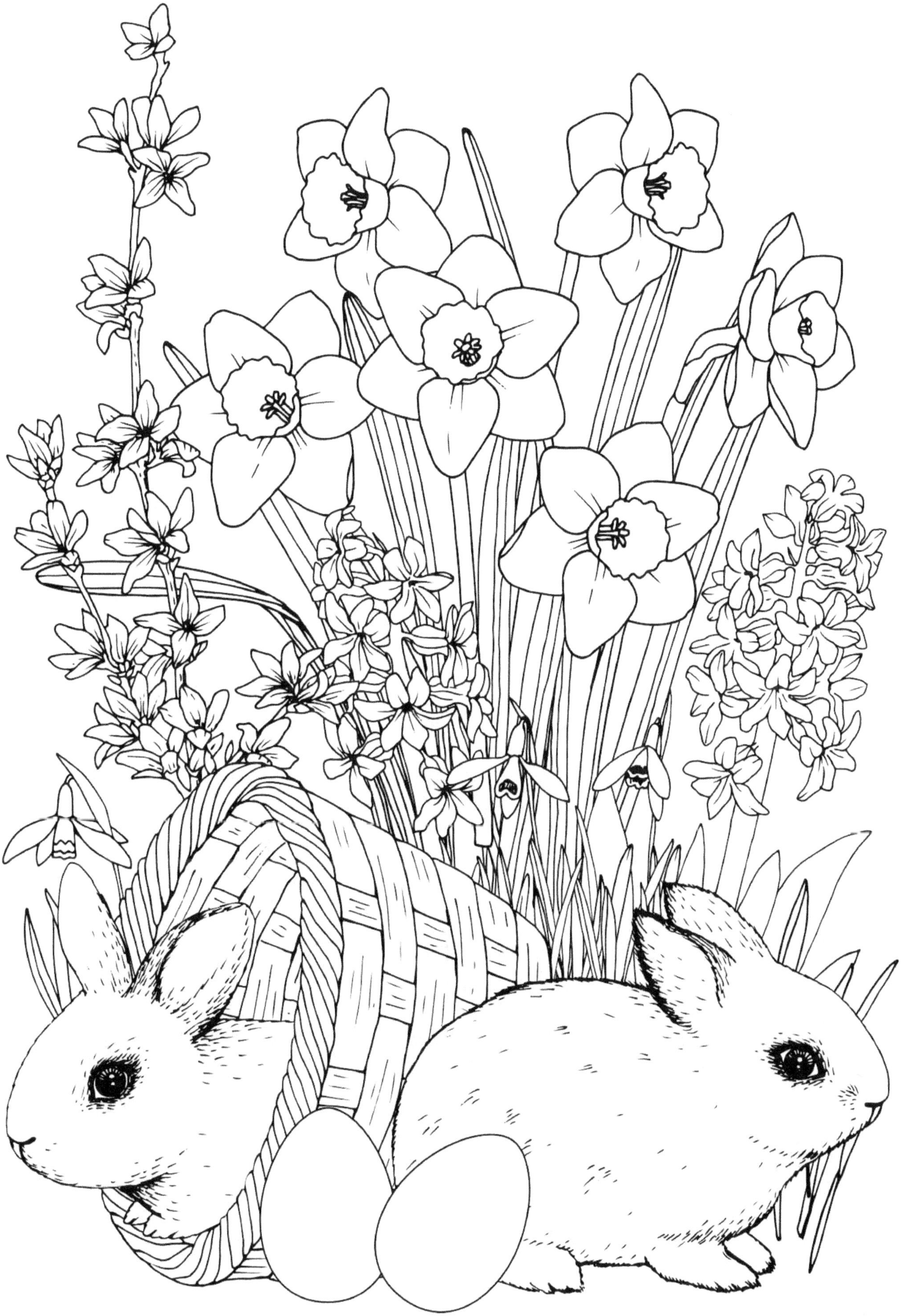

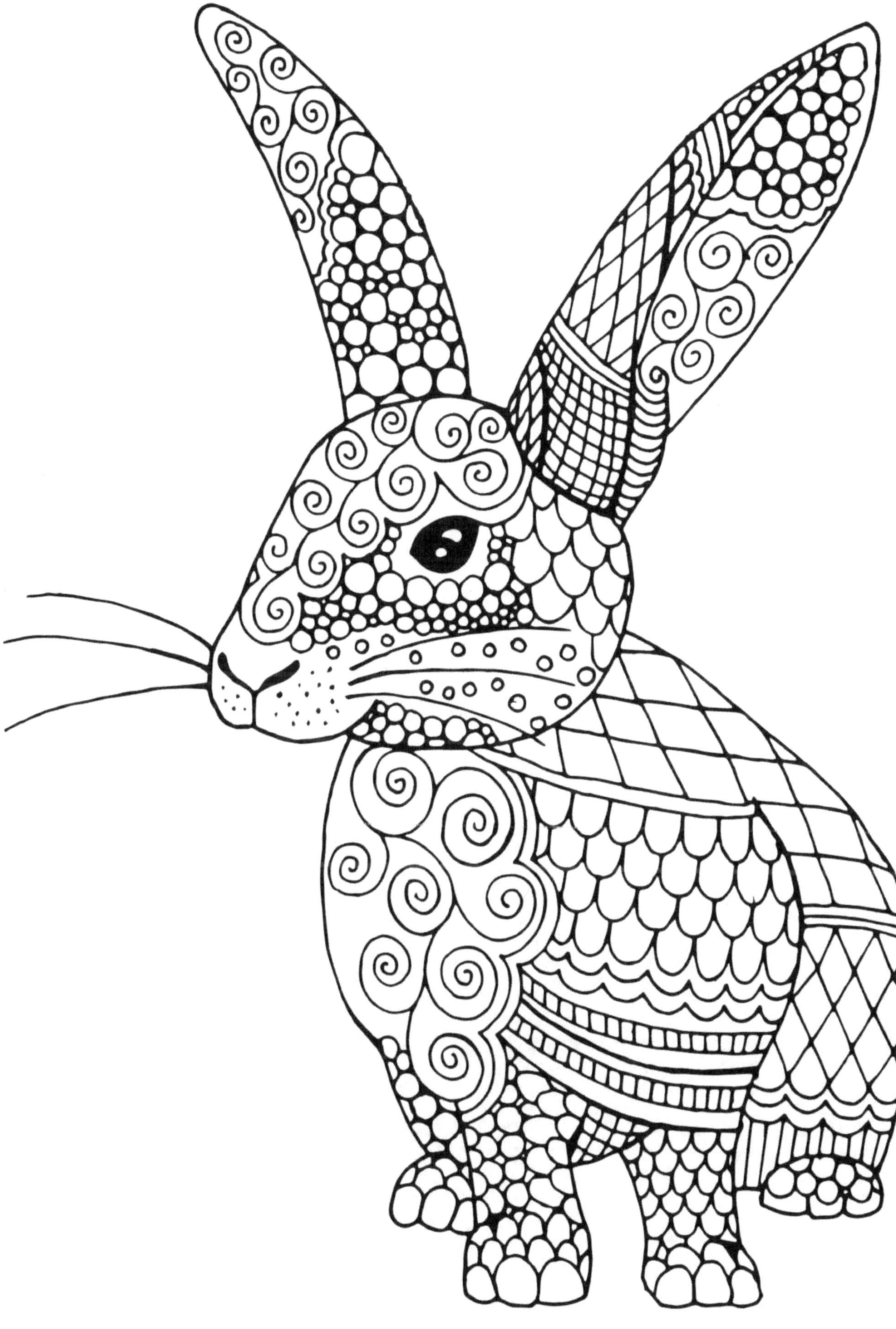

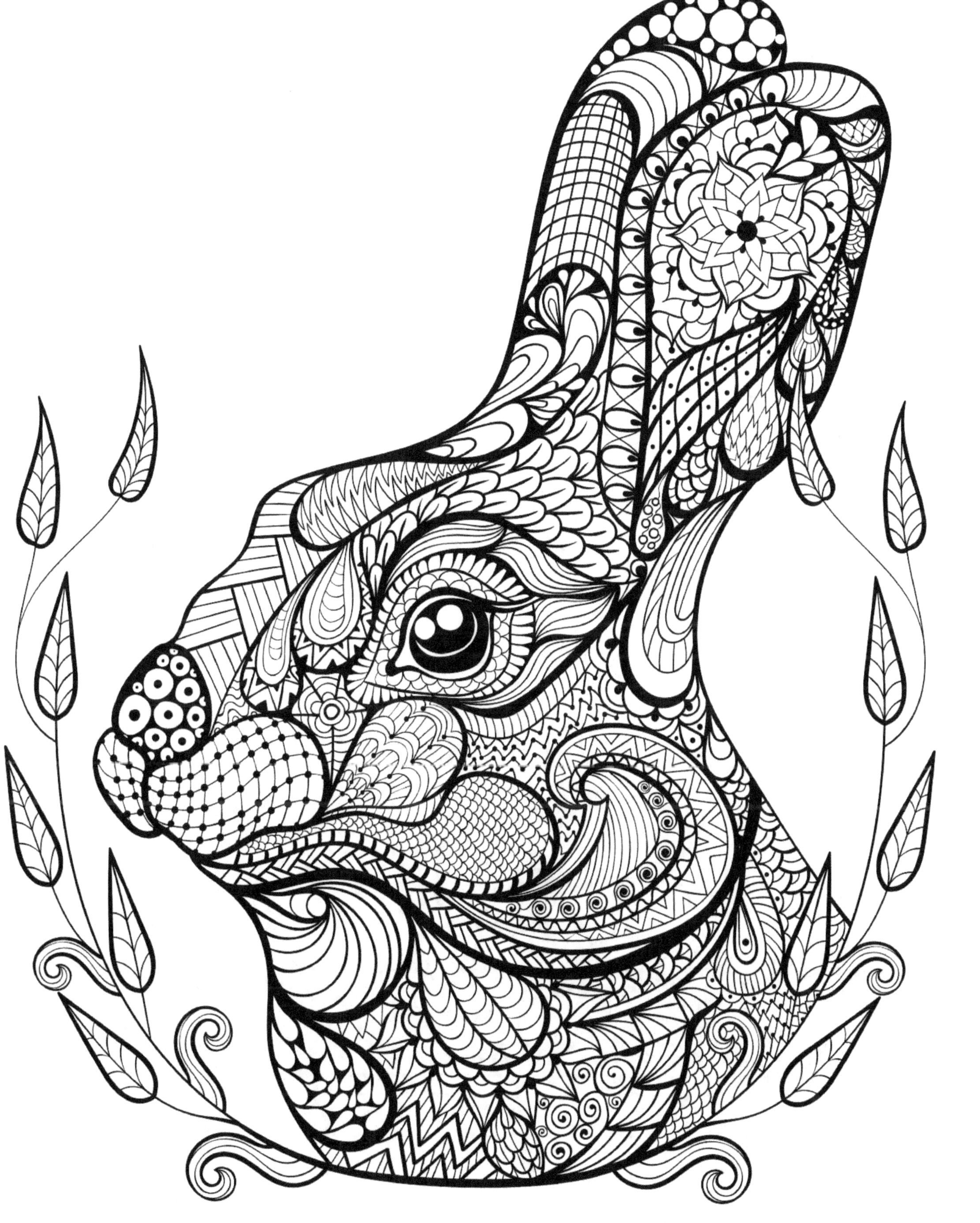

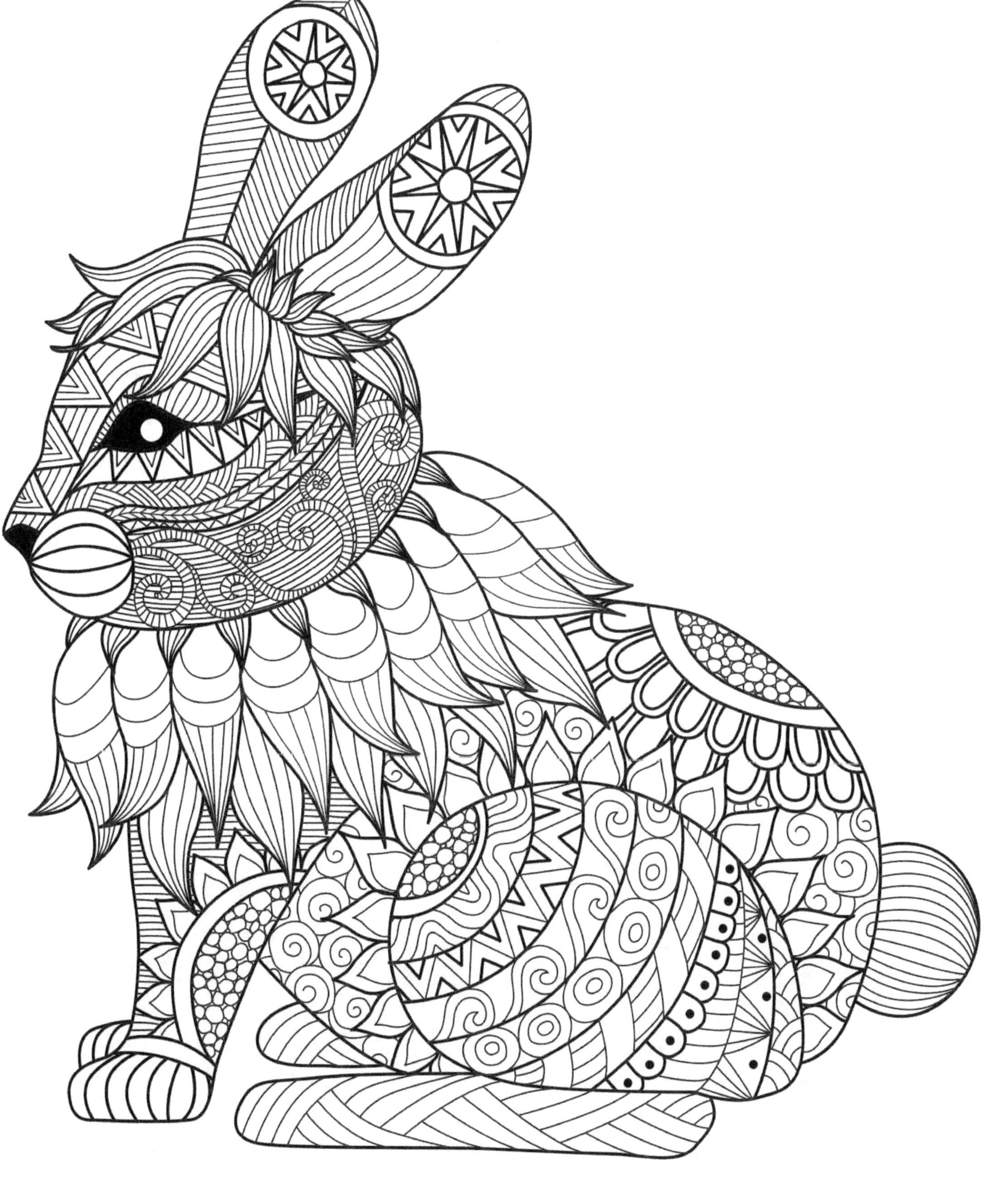

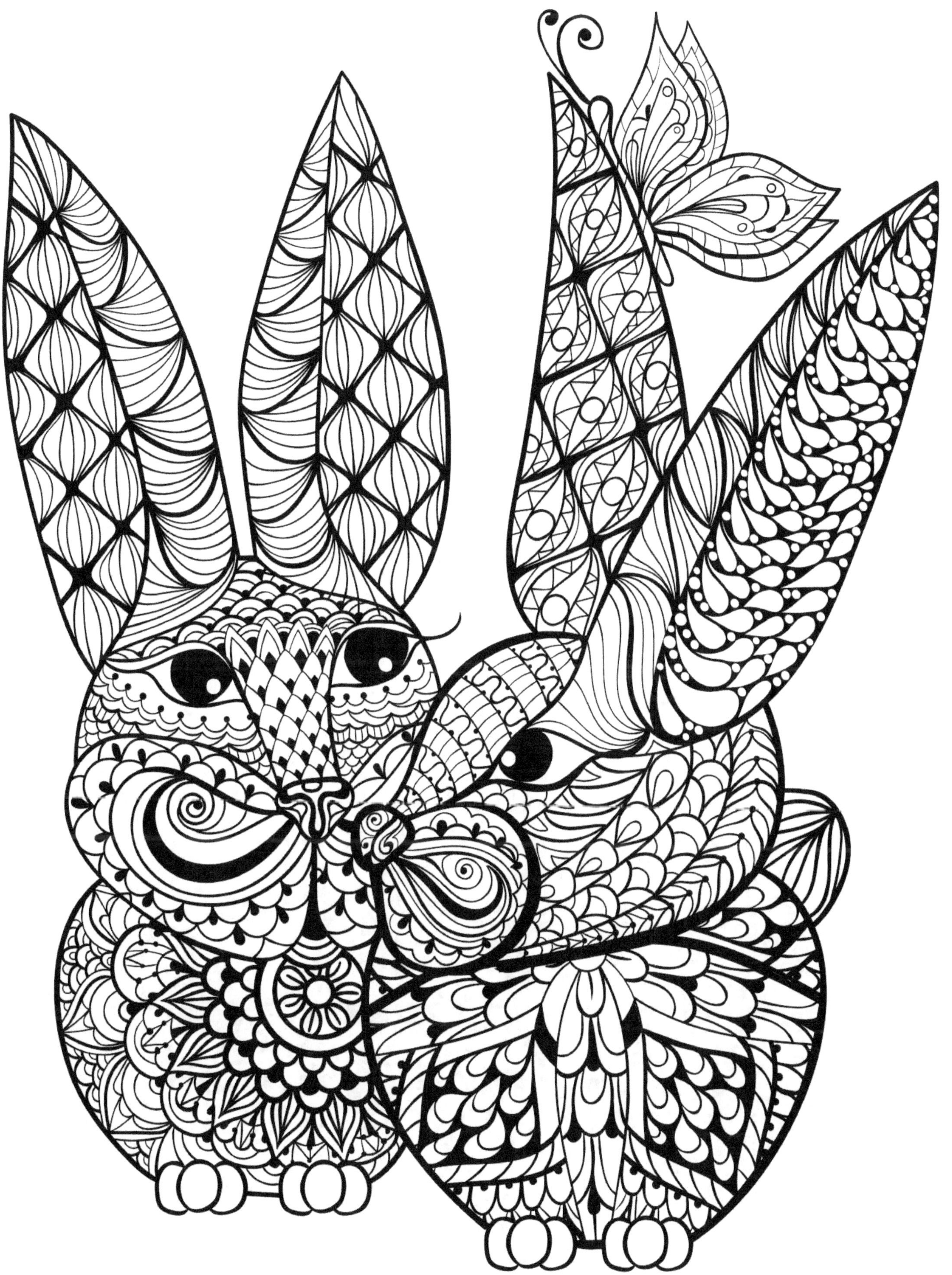

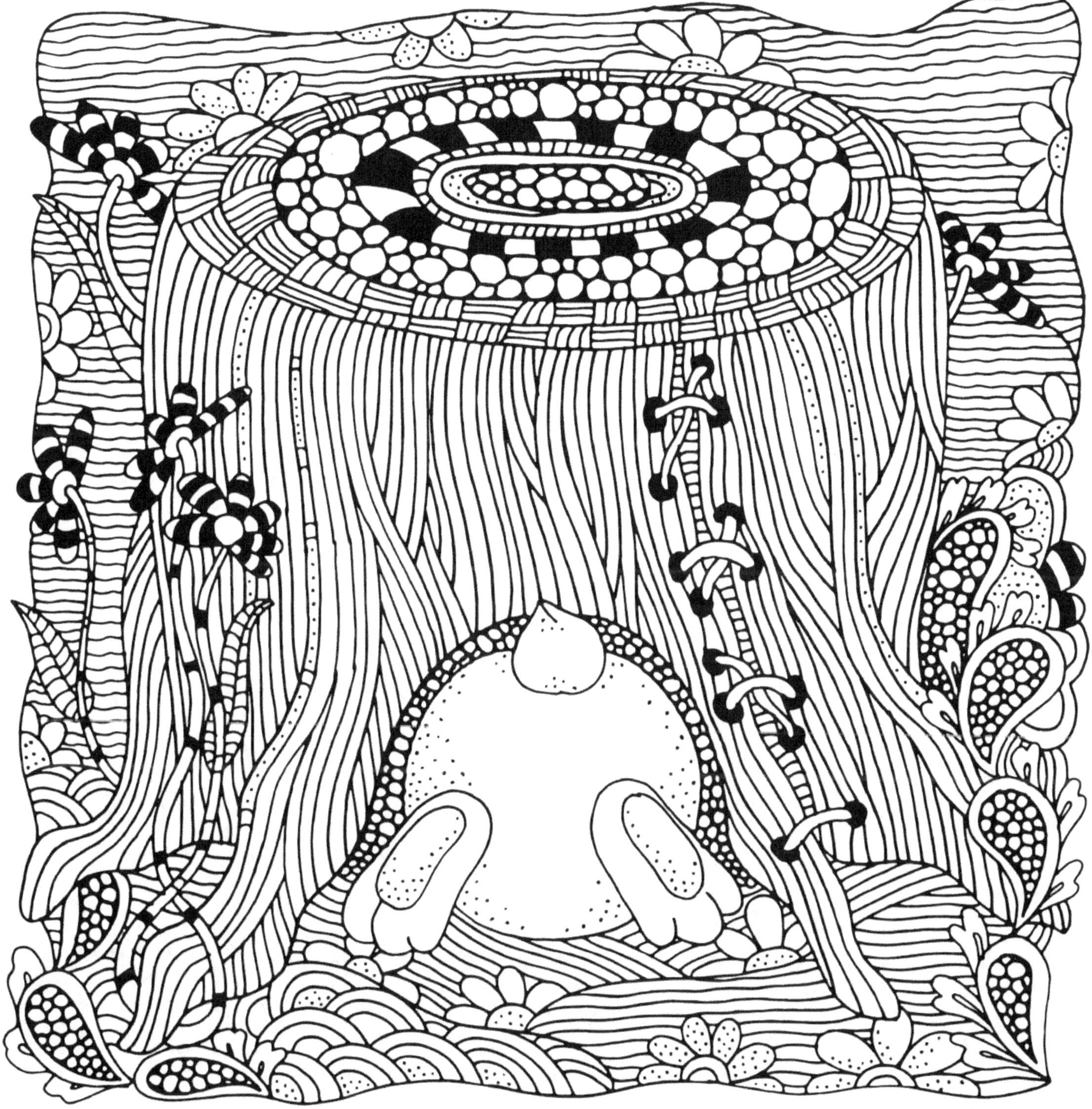

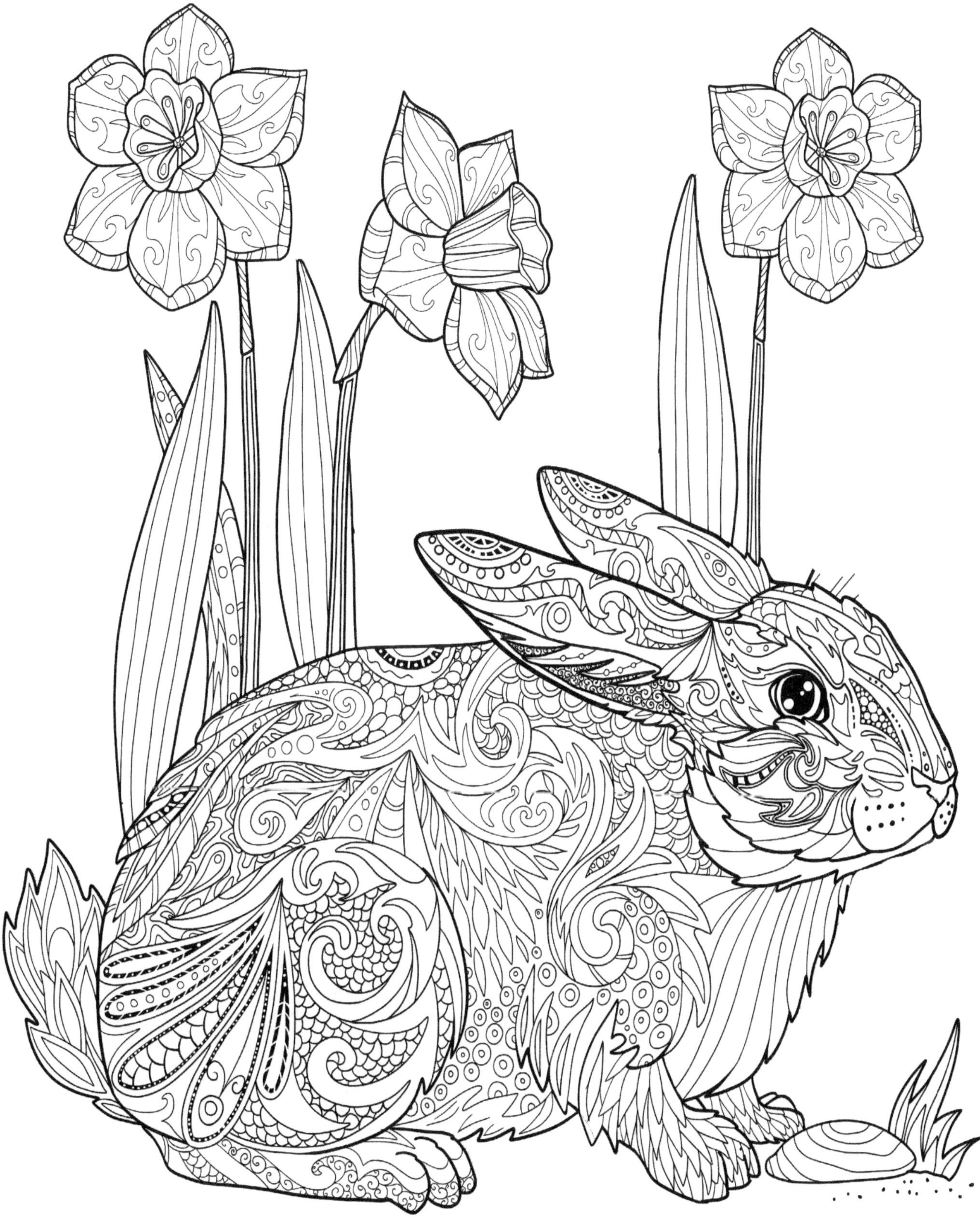

www.ingramcontent.com/pod-product-compliance
Lightning Source LLC
Chambersburg PA
CBHW062231220526
45471CB00009B/3435
9781986023290